ROWAN

purelife

18 designs by Marie Wallin
in Rowan Purelife
organic cotton – naturally dyed

why organic? this **eco-responsible** yarn uses fully certified organic cotton which keeps **nature pure** and **life good** for the farmers who make their living from the earth – each batch of cotton can be traced back to the certified farms in India where the cotton has been grown **how does this benefit the farmer?** farmers get a fairprice for the cotton which helps them increase their incomes and reduce their debts **what about the environment?** our organic cotton is grown in an environmentally and socially responsible way without the use of pesticides and chemical fertilizers – we are **using organic plant dyes** which produce no toxic effluent

wallflower pattern page 42

morning glory pattern page 44

mallow pattern page 46

love in a mist pattern page 50

candytuft pattern page 52

moonflower pattern page 54

buttercup pattern page 48

carnation pattern page 56

cherry pie (right) pattern page 57
sweet william (left) pattern page 62

cherry pie *pattern page 57*

sweet william *pattern page 62*

woodruff *pattern page 59*

cedar pattern page 64

cornflower pattern page 75

busy lizzie (left) pattern page 66
ash (right) pattern page 74

snapdragon *pattern page 68*

sycamore pattern page 70

oak pattern page 72

The Yarn

Our organically grown naturally dyed yarn knits to standard DK tension. The yarn is coloured with plant dyes and due to their organic nature some shade variation will simply add to the yarn's unique inherent beauty. To ensure the longevity of the yarn, avoid prolonged exposure to direct sunlight and follow the recommended wash care instructions found on the ball band. These natural variations do not in any way affect the quality or efficiency of the yarn.

The Colours

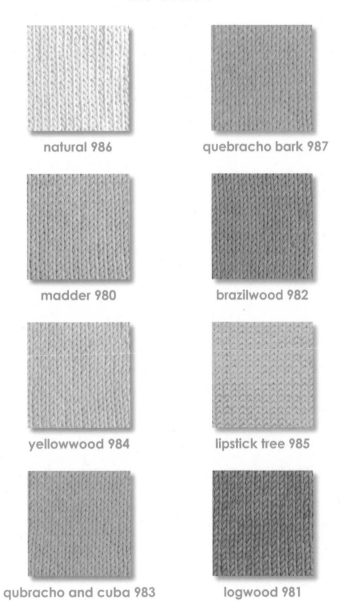

natural 986

quebracho bark 987

madder 980

brazilwood 982

yellowwood 984

lipstick tree 985

qubracho and cuba 983

logwood 981

The Dyes

Annatto (Lipstick Tree)
This red dye is produced from the pulped fruit of a plant indigenous to the Caribbean, Central and South America It is also used for colouring dairy products and confectionery and was once used to treat fevers and kidney diseases.

Logwood
The chipped and fermented wood grown in tropical America is used in dyeing violets, blues, greys and black. It is also a mild astringent and is used in treating chronic dysentery.

Madder
A prickly herb from Southern Europe which is used as fodder for animals and whose root can be powdered up to produce many shades of red. Reputed to help in cases of jaundice.

Brazilwood
New World heartwood which gives a true red dye, and revolutionised the world of 16th Century fashion.

Yellowwood/Cubawood
Trees that have yellow heartwood and which can be used for dyeing browns, black and yellow. The bark can also be used to make a gargle for sore throats.

Quebracho
A tall evergreen tree from South America with particularly dense 'axe breaker' wood. It is a natural source of tannin and in some cases can be used to help asthma and emphysema.

Biore

Rowan Purelife organic cotton is fully certified by **Biore** (part of the Swiss group Remei). **Biore** was founded 25 years ago with a company ethos of – **everyone has the right to work and live with dignity**.

Biore supports, through its foundation, the whole organic farming community, funding mobile health units, malaria prevention, and schooling for the children and hand pumps for drinking water. **Biore** also outlaws child labour, regulates working hours and sets a minimum wage. **Biore** also guarantees to buy the farmers cotton for 5 consecutive years at 20% above the standard price paid for conventional cotton.

Sizing Guide

Standard Sizing Guide for Women

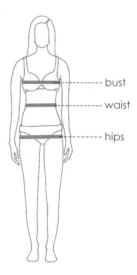
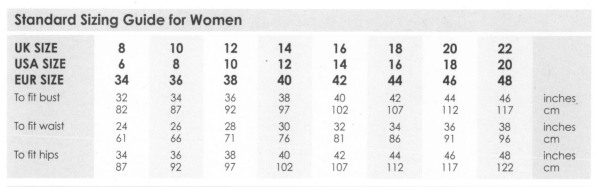

bust
waist
hips

UK SIZE	8	10	12	14	16	18	20	22	
USA SIZE	6	8	10	12	14	16	18	20	
EUR SIZE	34	36	38	40	42	44	46	48	
To fit bust	32	34	36	38	40	42	44	46	inches
	82	87	92	97	102	107	112	117	cm
To fit waist	24	26	28	30	32	34	36	38	inches
	61	66	71	76	81	86	91	96	cm
To fit hips	34	36	38	40	42	44	46	48	inches
	87	92	97	102	107	112	117	122	cm

Casual Sizing Guide for Women

As there are some designs are intended to fit more generously, we have introduced our casual sizing guide. The designs that fall into this group can be recognised by the size range: Small, Medium, Large and Extra Large. Each of these sizes cover 2 sizes from the standard sizing guide, ie. Size S will fit sizes 8/10, size M will fit size 12/14 and so on.

The sizing within this chart is based on the larger size within the range, ie. M will be based on size 14

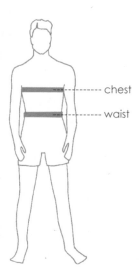

chest
waist

UK SIZE	S	M	L	XL	
DUAL SIZE	8/10	12/14	16/18	20/22	
To fit bust	32 – 34	36 – 38	40 – 42	44 – 46	inches
	82 – 87	92 – 97	102 – 107	112 – 117	cm
To fit waist	24 – 26	28 – 30	32 – 34	36 – 38	inches
	61 – 66	71 – 76	81 – 86	91 – 96	cm
To fit hips	34 – 36	38 – 40	42 – 44	46 – 48	inches
	87 – 92	97 – 102	107 – 112	117 – 122	cm

Standard Sizing Guide for Men

UK SIZE	S	M	L	XL	XXL	
EUR SIZE	50	52	54	56	58	
To fit chest	40	42	44	46	48	inches
	102	107	112	117	122	cm
To fit waist	32	34	36	38	40	inches
	81	86	91	96	101	cm

Standard Sizing Guide for Children

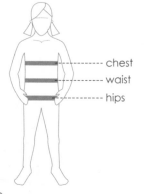

chest
waist
hips

The sizing within this chart is based on the larger size within the range, ie. age 3 – 4 yrs will be based on age 4 yrs

AGE	3 – 4 yrs	5 – 6 yrs	7 – 8 yrs	9 – 10 yrs	11 – 12 yrs	
To fit height	38.5 – 41	43.25 – 45.5	48 – 50.25	52.75 – 55	57.5 – 60	inches
	98 – 104	110 – 116	122 – 128	134 – 140	146 – 152	cm
To fit chest	21.5 – 22.5	23 – 24	25 – 26.5	27 – 28.75	29.5 – 31	inches
	55 – 57	59 – 61	63 – 67	69 – 73	75 – 79	cm
To fit waist	21 – 21.25	21.5 – 22.25	23 – 23.75	24 – 25	25 – 27	inches
	53 – 54	55 – 57	58 – 60	61 – 64	64 – 68	cm
To fit hips	23 – 23.75	24.5 – 25.5	26.75 – 28	28.75 – 30.75	31 – 33	inches
	58 – 60	62 – 65	68 – 71	73 – 78	79 – 84	cm

The Gallery

wallflower
main image page 4
pattern page 42

morning glory
main image page 7
pattern page 44

mallow
main image page 9
pattern page 46

love in a mist
main image page 10
pattern page 50

candytuft
main image page 12
pattern page 52

moonflower
main image page 14
pattern page 54

buttercup
main image page 16
pattern page 48

carnation
main image page 18
pattern page 56

cherry pie
main image page 22
pattern page 57

sweet william
main image page 23
pattern page 62

woodruff
main image page 25
pattern page 59

cedar
main image page 26
pattern page 64

cornflower
main image page 27
pattern page 75

busy lizzie
main image page 29
pattern page 66

ash
main image page 29
pattern page 74

snapdragon
main image page 31
pattern page 68

sycamore
main image page 33
pattern page 70

oak
main image page 34
pattern page 72

41

wallflower

main image page 4

SIZE

	S	M	L	XL	
To fit bust					
	81-86	91-97	102-107	112-117	cm
	32-34	36-38	40-42	44-46	in

YARN

Rowan Purelife Organic Cotton

12	13	15	16	x 50gm

(photographed in Madder 980)

NEEDLES

1 pair 3¹/4mm (no 10) (US 3) needles
1 pair 3³/4mm (no 9) (US 5) needles
3¹/4mm (no 10) (US 3) circular needle
Cable needle

TENSION

26 sts and 30 rows to 10 cm measured over patt using 3³/4mm (US 5) needles.

SPECIAL ABBREVIATIONS

Cr2R = slip next st onto cable needle and leave at back of work, K1, then P1 from cable needle;
Cr2L = slip next st onto cable needle and leave at front of work, P1, then K1 from cable needle.

BACK

Using 3¹/4mm (US 3) needles cast on 94 [106: 120: 134] sts.
Work in g st for 8 rows, ending with RS facing for next row.
Row 9 (RS): K3 [3: 5: 6], M1, (K5, M1, K6, M1) 8 [9: 10: 11] times, K to end. 111 [125: 141: 157] sts.
Change to 3³/4mm (US 5) needles.
Cont in patt as folls:
Row 1 (WS): K1 [2: 4: 0], P1, *K4, P3, K4, P1, rep from * to last 1 [2: 4: 0] sts, K1 [2: 4: 0].
Row 2: P1 [2: 4: 0], K1, *P3, Cr2R, K1, Cr2L, P3, K1, rep from * to last 1 [2: 4: 0] sts, P1 [2: 4: 0].
Row 3: K1 [2: 4: 0], P1, *K3, (P1, K1) twice, P1, K3, P1, rep from * to last 1 [2: 4: 0] sts, K1 [2: 4: 0].
Row 4: P1 [2: 4: 0], K1, *P2, Cr2R, P1, K1, P1, Cr2L, P2, K1, rep from * to last 1 [2: 4: 0] sts, P1 [2: 4: 0].
Row 5: K1 [2: 4: 0], P1, *K2, P1, rep from * to last 1 [2: 4: 0] sts, K1 [2: 4: 0].
Row 6: P1 [2: 4: 0], K1, *P1, Cr2R, P2, K1, P2, Cr2L, P1, K1, rep from * to last 1 [2: 4: 0] sts, P1 [2: 4: 0].
Row 7: K1 [2: 4: 0], P1, *K1, P1, (K3, P1) twice, K1, P1, rep from * to last 1 [2: 4: 0] sts, K1 [2: 4: 0].
Row 8: P1 [2: 4: 0], K1, *Cr2R, P3, K1, P3, Cr2L, K1, rep from * to last 1 [2: 4: 0] sts, P1 [2: 4: 0].
These 8 rows form patt.
Cont in patt, dec 1 st at each end of next and 3 foll 4th rows. 103 [117: 133: 149] sts.
Cont straight until back meas 13 [14: 15: 16] cm, ending with RS facing for next row.
Inc 1 st at each end of next and 3 foll 10th rows, taking inc sts into patt. 111 [125: 141: 157] sts.
Work 17 rows, ending with RS facing for next row.
(Back should meas 29 [30: 31: 32] cm.)

Shape armholes

Keeping patt correct, cast off 4 [5: 6: 7] sts at beg of next 2 rows. 103 [115: 129: 143] sts.
Dec 1 st at each end of next 5 [7: 9: 11] rows, then on foll 4 [5: 6: 7] alt rows. 85 [91: 99: 107] sts.
Cont straight until armhole meas 17 [18: 19: 20] cm, ending with RS facing for next row.

Shape shoulders and back neck

Cast off 6 [7: 8: 9] sts at beg of next 2 rows. 73 [77: 83: 89] sts.
Next row (RS): Cast off 6 [7: 8: 9] sts, patt until there are 8 [9: 10: 12] sts on right needle and turn, leaving rem sts on a holder.
Work each side of neck separately.
Cast off 3 sts at beg of next row.
Cast off rem 5 [6: 7: 9] sts.
With RS facing, rejoin yarn to rem sts, cast off centre 45 [45: 47: 47] sts, K to end.
Complete to match first side, reversing shapings.

LEFT FRONT

Using 3¹/4mm (US 3) needles cast on 88 [99: 111: 129] sts.
Work in g st for 8 rows, ending with RS facing for next row.
Row 9 (RS): K3 [3: 3: 7], M1, (K5, M1, K6, M1) 7 [8: 9: 10] times, K to last 5 sts, M1 and turn, leaving rem 5 sts on a holder. 99 [112: 126: 146] sts.
Change to 3³/4mm (US 5) needles.
Cont in patt as folls:
Row 1 (WS): K1, P1, *K4, P3, K4, P1, rep from * to last 1 [2: 4: 0] sts, K1 [2: 4: 0].
Row 2: P1 [2: 4: 0], K1, *P3, Cr2R, K1, Cr2L, P3, K1, rep from * to last st, P1.
Row 3: K1, P1, *K3, (P1, K1) twice, P1, K3, P1, rep from * to last 1 [2: 4: 0] sts, K1 [2: 4: 0].
Row 4: P1 [2: 4: 0], K1, *P2, Cr2R, P1, K1, P1, Cr2L, P2, K1, rep from * to last st, P1.
Row 5: K1, P1, *K2, P1, rep from * to last 1 [2: 4: 0] sts, K1 [2: 4: 0].
Row 6: P1 [2: 4: 0], K1, *P1, Cr2R, P2, K1, P2, Cr2L, P1, K1, rep from * to last st, P1.
Row 7: K1, P1, *K1, P1, (K3, P1) twice, K1, P1, rep from * to last 1 [2: 4: 0] sts, K1 [2: 4: 0].
Row 8: P1 [2: 4: 0], K1, *Cr2R, P3, K1, P3, Cr2L, K1, rep from * to last st, P1.
These 8 rows form patt.
Cont in patt, dec 1 st at beg of next and 3 foll 4th rows. 95 [108: 122: 142] sts.
Cont straight until 10 rows less have been worked than on back to first side seam inc, ending with RS facing for next row.

Shape front slope

Keeping patt correct, dec 1 st at end of next row and at same edge on foll 40 [50: 57: 57] rows, then on foll 8 [3: 0: 0] alt rows **and at same time** inc 1 st at beg of 11th and 3 foll 10th rows. 50 [58: 68: 88] sts.
Work 1 [1: 0: 0] row, ending with RS facing for next row.

Shape armhole

Keeping patt correct, cast off 4 [5: 6: 7] sts at beg and dec 1 st at end of next row. 45 [52: 61: 80] sts.
Work 1 row, dec 0 [0: 1: 1] st at front slope edge. 45 [52: 60: 79] sts.
Dec 1 st at armhole edge of next 5 [7: 9: 11] rows, then on foll 4 [5: 6: 7] alt rows **and at same time** dec 1 st at front slope edge of next 1 [1: 1: 23] rows, then on foll 6 [8: 10: 1] alt rows. 29 [31: 34: 37] sts.
Dec 1 st at front slope edge **only** on 2nd and foll 8 [7: 7: 6] alt rows, then on 3 foll 4th rows.
17 [20: 23: 27] sts.

Cont straight until left front matches back to beg of shoulder shaping, ending with RS facing for next row.

Shape shoulder

Cast off 6 [7: 8: 9] sts at beg of next and foll alt row.
Work 1 row.
Cast off rem 5 [6: 7: 9] sts.

RIGHT FRONT

Using 3¼mm (US 3) needles cast on 88 [99: 111: 129] sts.
Work in g st for 8 rows, ending with RS facing for next row.

Row 9 (RS): K5 and slip these 5 sts onto a holder, M1, K3 [3: 3: 7], M1, (K5, M1, K6, M1) 7 [8: 9: 10] times, K to end. 99 [112: 126: 146] sts.
Change to 3¾mm (US 5) needles.
Cont in patt as folls:

Row 1 (WS): K1 [2: 4: 0], P1, *K4, P3, K4, P1, rep from * to last st, K1.

Row 2: P1, K1, *P3, Cr2R, K1, Cr2L, P3, K1, rep from * to last 1 [2: 4: 0] sts, P1 [2: 4: 0].

Row 3: K1 [2: 4: 0], P1, *K3, (P1, K1) twice, P1, K3, P1, rep from * to last st, K1.

Row 4: P1, K1, *P2, Cr2R, P1, K1, P1, Cr2L, P2, K1, rep from * to last 1 [2: 4: 0] sts, P1 [2: 4: 0].

Row 5: K1 [2: 4: 0], P1, *K2, P1, rep from * to last st, K1.

Row 6: P1, K1, *P1, Cr2R, P2, K1, P2, Cr2L, P1, K1, rep from * to last 1 [2: 4: 0] sts, P1 [2: 4: 0].

Row 7: K1 [2: 4: 0], P1, *K1, P1, (K3, P1) twice, K1, P1, rep from * to last st, K1.

Row 8: P1, K1, *Cr2R, P3, K1, P3, Cr2L, K1, rep from * to last 1 [2: 4: 0] sts, P1 [2: 4: 0].
These 8 rows form patt.
Cont in patt, dec 1 st at end of next and 3 foll 4th rows. 95 [108: 122: 142] sts.
Complete to match left front, reversing shapings.

SLEEVES

Using 3¼mm (US 3) needles cast on 64 sts.
Work in g st for 8 rows, ending with RS facing for next row.

Row 9 (RS): K4, M1, (K5, M1, K6, M1) 5 times, K to end. 75 sts.
Change to 3¾mm (US 5) needles.
Cont in patt as folls:

Row 1 (WS): K1, P1, *K4, P3, K4, P1, rep from * to last st, K1.

Row 2: P1, K1, *P3, Cr2R, K1, Cr2L, P3, K1, rep from * to last st, P1.

Row 3: K1, P1, *K3, (P1, K1) twice, P1, K3, P1, rep from * to last st, K1.

Row 4: P1, K1, *P2, Cr2R, P1, K1, P1, Cr2L, P2, K1, rep from * to last st, P1.

Row 5: K1, P1, *K2, P1, rep from * to last st, K1.

Row 6: P1, K1, *P1, Cr2R, P2, K1, P2, Cr2L, P1, K1, rep from * to last st, P1.

Row 7: K1, P1, *K1, P1, (K3, P1) twice, K1, P1, rep from * to last st, K1.

Row 8: P1, K1, *Cr2R, P3, K1, P3, Cr2L, K1, rep from * to last st, P1.
These 8 rows form patt.
Work in patt until sleeve meas 15 cm, ending with RS facing for next row.
Cont in patt, shaping sides by inc 1 st at each end of next and every foll 8th [6th: 6th: 4th] row to 95 [89: 103: 89] sts, then on every foll – [8th: –: 6th] row until there are – [99: –: 107] sts, taking inc sts into patt.
Cont straight until sleeve meas 44 [45: 46: 46] cm, ending with RS facing for next row.

Shape top

Keeping patt correct, cast off 4 [5: 6: 7] sts at beg of next 2 rows. 87 [89: 91: 93] sts.
Dec 1 st at each end of next 5 rows, then on every foll alt row to 71 sts, then on foll 13 rows, ending with RS facing for next row. 45 sts.
Cast off 4 sts at beg of next 6 rows.
Cast off rem 21 sts.

MAKING UP

Press as described on the information page.
Join both shoulder seams using back stitch, or mattress stitch if preferred.

Left front opening band

Slip 5 sts from left front holder onto 3¼mm (US 3) needles and rejoin yarn with RS facing.
Cont in g st until band, when slightly stretched, fits up left front opening edge to beg of front slope shaping, ending with RS facing for next row.
Break yarn and leave sts on a holder.
Slip st band in place.

Right front opening band

Slip 5 sts from right front holder onto 3¼mm (US 3) needles and rejoin yarn with **WS** facing.
Cont in g st until band, when slightly stretched, fits up right front opening edge to beg of front slope shaping, ending with RS facing for next row.
Do NOT break yarn.
Slip st band in place.

Front band

With RS facing and using 3¼mm (US 3) circular needle, K 5 sts of right front opening band, pick up and knit 110 [112: 116: 118] sts up right front slope, 51 [51: 53: 53] sts from back, and 110 [112: 116: 118] sts down left front slope, then K 5 sts of left front opening band. 281 [285: 295: 299] sts.
Work in g st for 8 rows, ending with **WS** facing for next row.
Cast off knitwise (on WS).
See information page for finishing instructions, setting in sleeves using the set-in method and leaving a small opening in right side seam level with beg of front slope shaping.

Ties (make 2)

Using 3¼mm (US 3) needles cast on 5 sts.
Work in g st until tie meas 100 [105: 110: 115] cm, ending with RS facing for next row.
Cast off.
Attach cast-on ends of ties to front opening row-end edges so that one edge of tie matches cast-off edge of front band.

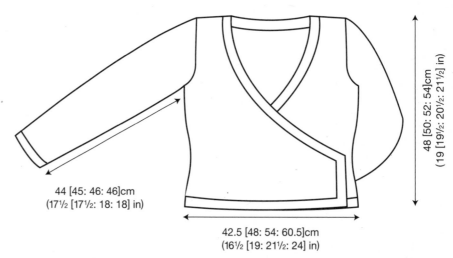

44 [45: 46: 46]cm
(17½ [17½: 18: 18] in)

42.5 [48: 54: 60.5]cm
(16½ [19: 21½: 24] in)

48 [50: 52: 54]cm
(19 [19½: 20½: 21½] in)

morning glory 🌱

main image page 7

SIZE

8	10	12	14	16	18	20	22	
To fit bust								
81	86	91	97	102	107	112	117	in
32	34	36	38	40	42	44	46	cm

YARN

Rowan Purelife Organic Cotton

10	10	11	12	12	13	13	14	x 50gm

(photographed in Quebracho and Cuba 983)

NEEDLES

1 pair 3¹⁄₄mm (no 10) (US 3) needles
1 pair 3³⁄₄mm (no 9) (US 5) needles

BUTTONS

6 x 00409

TENSION

22 sts and 30 rows to 10 cm measured over st st
using 3³⁄₄mm (US 5) needles.

BACK

Using 3¹⁄₄mm (US 3) needles cast on 97 [101: 105: 113: 119: 125: 133: 139] sts.

Work in g st for 12 rows, ending with RS facing for next row.

Change to 3³⁄₄mm (US 5) needles.

Beg with a K row, work in st st for 20 rows, ending with RS facing for next row.

Counting in from both ends of last row, place markers on 25th [26th: 27th: 29th: 30th: 32nd: 34th: 35th] sts in from both ends of last row.

Row 33 (dec row) (RS): K2, sl 1, K1, psso, *K to within 2 sts of marked st, K2tog, K marked st, sl 1, K1, psso, rep from * once more, K to last 4 sts, K2tog, K2.

Work 11 rows.

Rep last 12 rows once more, then first of these rows (the dec row) again.

79 [83: 87: 95: 101: 107: 115: 121] sts.

Work 19 rows, ending with RS facing for next row.

Next row (inc row) (RS): K2, M1, *K to within 1 st of marked st, M1, K3 (marked st is 2nd of these 3 sts), M1, rep from * once more, K to last 2 sts, M1, K2.

Work 11 rows.

Rep last 12 rows once more, then first of these rows (the inc row) again.

97 [101: 105: 113: 119: 125: 133: 139] sts.

Cont straight until back meas 41 [41: 40: 43: 42: 44: 43: 45] cm, ending with RS facing for next row.

Shape armholes

Cast off 3 [4: 4: 5: 5: 6: 6: 7] sts at beg of next 2 rows.

91 [93: 97: 103: 109: 113: 121: 125] sts.

Dec 1 st at each end of next 5 [5: 7: 7: 9: 9: 11: 11]

rows, then on foll 4 [4: 3: 4: 4: 4: 4: 5] alt rows.

73 [75: 77: 81: 83: 87: 91: 93] sts.

Cont straight until armhole meas 18 [18: 19: 19: 20: 20: 21: 21] cm, ending with RS facing for next row.

Shape shoulders and back neck

Cast off 6 [6: 7: 7: 7: 8: 9: 9] sts at beg of next 2 rows. 61 [63: 63: 67: 69: 71: 73: 75] sts.

Next row (RS): Cast off 6 [6: 7: 7: 7: 8: 9: 9] sts, K until there are 9 [10: 9: 11: 11: 11: 11: 12] sts on right needle and turn, leaving rem sts on a holder.

Work each side of neck separately.

Cast off 3 sts at beg of next row.

Cast off rem 6 [7: 6: 8: 8: 8: 8: 9] sts.

With RS facing, rejoin yarn to rem sts, cast off centre 31 [31: 31: 31: 33: 33: 33: 33] sts, K to end.

Complete to match first side, reversing shapings.

LEFT FRONT

Using 3¹⁄₄mm (US 3) needles cast on 52 [54: 56: 60: 63: 66: 70: 73] sts.

Work in g st for 11 rows, ending with **WS** facing for next row.

Row 12 (WS): K7 and slip these 7 sts onto a holder, M1, K to end. 46 [48: 50: 54: 57: 60: 64: 67] sts.

Change to 3³⁄₄mm (US 5) needles.

Beg with a K row, work in st st for 20 rows, ending with RS facing for next row.

Counting in from end of last row, place marker on 25th [26th: 27th: 29th: 30th: 32nd: 34th: 35th] st in from end of last row.

Row 33 (dec row) (RS): K2, sl 1, K1, psso, K to within 2 sts of marked st, K2tog, K marked st, sl 1, K1, psso, K to end.

Work 11 rows.

Rep last 12 rows once more, then first of these rows (the dec row) again. 37 [39: 41: 45: 48: 51: 55: 58] sts.

Work 19 rows, ending with RS facing for next row.

Next row (inc row) (RS): K2, M1, K to within 1 st of marked st, M1, K3 (marked st is 2nd of these 3 sts), M1, K to end.

Work 11 rows.

Rep last 12 rows once more, then first of these rows (the inc row) again. 46 [48: 50: 54: 57: 60: 64: 67] sts.

Cont straight until left front matches back to beg of armhole shaping, ending with RS facing for next row.

Shape armhole

Cast off 3 [4: 4: 5: 5: 6: 6: 7] sts at beg of next row.

43 [44: 46: 49: 52: 54: 58: 60] sts.

Work 1 row.

Dec 1 st at armhole edge of next 5 [5: 7: 7: 9: 9: 11: 11] rows, then on foll 4 [4: 3: 4: 4: 4: 4: 5] alt rows.

34 [35: 36: 38: 39: 41: 43: 44] sts.

Cont straight until 17 [17: 17: 19: 19: 19: 21: 21] rows less have been worked than on back to beg of shoulder shaping, ending with **WS** facing for next row.

Shape neck

Cast off 7 [7: 7: 6: 7: 7: 6: 6] sts at beg of next row.

27 [28: 29: 32: 32: 34: 37: 38] sts.

Dec 1 st at neck edge of next 5 rows, then on foll 4 [4: 4: 5: 5: 5: 6: 6] alt rows.

18 [19: 20: 22: 22: 24: 26: 27] sts.

Work 3 rows, ending with RS facing for next row.

Shape shoulder

Cast off 6 [6: 7: 7: 7: 8: 9: 9] sts at beg of next and foll alt row.

Work 1 row.

Cast off rem 6 [7: 6: 8: 8: 8: 8: 9] sts.

RIGHT FRONT

Using 3¼mm (US 3) needles cast on 52 [54: 56: 60: 63: 66: 70: 73] sts.

Work in g st for 11 rows, ending with **WS** facing for next row.

Row 12 (WS): K to last 7 sts, M1 and turn, leaving rem 7 sts on a holder.

46 [48: 50: 54: 57: 60: 64: 67] sts.

Change to 3¾mm (US 5) needles.

Beg with a K row, work in st st for 20 rows, ending with RS facing for next row.

Counting in from beg of last row, place marker on 25th [26th: 27th: 29th: 30th: 32nd: 34th: 35th] st in from beg of last row.

Row 33 (dec row) (RS): K to within 2 sts of marked st, K2tog, K marked st, sl 1, K1, psso, K to last 4 sts, K2tog, K2.

Complete to match left front, reversing shapings.

SLEEVES

Using 3¼mm (US 3) needles cast on 45 [45: 47: 47: 49: 49: 51: 51] sts.

Work in g st, inc 1 st at each end of 13th and every foll 6th [4th: 4th: 4th: 4th: 4th: 4th: 4th] row to 55 [53: 53: 59: 57: 63: 65: 65] sts, then on every foll – [6th: 6th: 6th: 6th: -: -: -] row to – [57: 59: 61: 61: -: -: -] sts.

Work 3 [3: 1: 1: 3: 3: 3: 3] rows, ending with RS facing for next row.

Change to 3¾mm (US 5) needles.

Beg with a K row, work in st st, shaping sides by inc 1 st at each end of 3rd [3rd: 5th: 5th: 3rd: 3rd: next: next] and every foll 6th [6th: 6th: 6th: 6th: 6th: 4th: 4th] row to 85 [87: 89: 91: 93: 95: 69: 75] sts, then on every foll – [-: -: -: -: -: 6th: 6th] row until there are – [-: -: -: -: -: 97: 99] sts.

Cont straight until sleeve meas 44 [44: 45: 45: 46: 46: 45: 45] cm, ending with RS facing for next row.

Shape top

Cast off 3 [4: 4: 5: 5: 6: 6: 7] sts at beg of next 2 rows. 79 [79: 81: 81: 83: 83: 85: 85] sts.

Dec 1 st at each end of next 5 rows, then on every foll alt row to 57 sts, then on foll 11 rows, ending with RS facing for next row. 35 sts.

Cast off 6 sts at beg of next 2 rows.

Cast off rem 23 sts.

MAKING UP

Press as described on the information page.

Join both shoulder seams using back stitch, or mattress stitch if preferred.

Button band

Slip 7 sts from left front holder onto 3¼mm (US 3) needles and rejoin yarn with RS facing.

Cont in g st until band, when slightly stretched, fits up left front opening edge to neck shaping, ending with **WS** facing for next row.

Cast off knitwise (on **WS**).

Slip st band in place.

Mark positions for 6 buttons on this band – first to come 15 cm up from cast-on edge, last to come 2 cm below neck shaping and rem 4 buttons evenly spaced between.

Buttonhole band

Slip 7 sts from right front holder onto 3¼mm (US 3) needles and rejoin yarn with **WS** facing.

Cont in g st until band, when slightly stretched, fits up right front opening edge to neck shaping, ending with **WS** facing for next row and making 6 buttonholes to correspond with positions marked for buttons as folls:

Buttonhole row (RS): K2, K2tog, yfwd, K3.

When band is complete, cast off knitwise (on **WS**).

Slip st band in place.

Collar

Using 3¼mm (US 3) needles cast on 112 [112: 112: 114: 118: 118: 122: 122] sts.

Work in g st for 8 cm, ending with RS facing for next row.

Cast off 3 sts at beg of next 24 rows.

Cast off rem 40 [40: 40: 42: 46: 46: 50: 50] sts.

Positioning ends of collar half way across top of bands, sew shaped cast-off edge of collar to neck edge.

Pockets (make 2)

Using 3¾mm (US 5) needles cast on 21 [21: 21: 23: 23: 23: 25: 25] sts.

Row 1 (RS): Knit.

Row 2: K1, P to last st, K1.

Row 3: K1, M1, K to last st, M1, K1.

Row 4: K1, P to last st, K1.

Rows 5 to 8: As rows 3 and 4, twice. 27 [27: 27: 29: 29: 29: 31: 31] sts.

Rows 9 to 30: As rows 1 and 2, 11 times.

Change to 3¼mm (US 3) needles.

Work in g st for 11 rows, ending with **WS** facing for next row.

Cast off knitwise (on **WS**).

See information page for finishing instructions, setting in sleeves using the set-in method. Using photograph as a guide, sew pockets onto fronts.

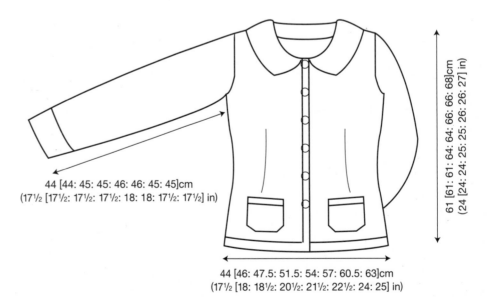

44 [44: 45: 45: 46: 46: 45: 45]cm
(17½ [17½: 17½: 17½: 18: 18: 17½: 17½] in)

61 [61: 61: 64: 64: 66: 66: 68]cm
(24 [24: 24: 25: 25: 26: 26: 27] in)

44 [46: 47.5: 51.5: 54: 57: 60.5: 63]cm
(17½ [18: 18½: 20½: 21½: 22½: 24: 25] in)

mallow

main image page 9

SIZE								
8	10	12	14	16	18	20	22	
To fit bust								
81	86	91	97	102	107	112	117	in
32	34	36	38	40	42	44	46	cm

YARN

Rowan Purelife Organic Cotton

9	9	10	10	11	11	12	13	x 50gm

(photographed in Brazilwood 982)

NEEDLES

1 pair 3¼mm (no 10) (US 3) needles
1 pair 3¾mm (no 9) (US 5) needles

BUTTONS

3 x 00417

TENSION

22 sts and 30 rows to 10 cm measured over st st
using 3¾mm (US 5) needles.

BACK

Using 3¼mm (US 3) needles cast on 93 [97: 101: 109: 115: 121: 129: 135] sts.

Row 1 (RS): K1 [1: 1: 1: 0: 1: 1: 0], *P1, K1, rep from * to last 0 [0: 0: 0: 1: 0: 0: 1] st, P0 [0: 0: 0: 1: 0: 0: 1].

Row 2: As row 1.

These 2 rows form moss st.

Work in moss st for a further 6 rows, ending with RS facing for next row.

Change to 3¾mm (US 5) needles.

Beg and ending rows as indicated and repeating the 14 row patt repeat throughout, cont in patt from chart as folls:

Dec 1 st at each end of 3rd and every foll 4th row until 83 [87: 91: 99: 105: 111: 119: 125] sts rem.

Work 11 rows, ending with RS facing for next row.

Inc 1 st at each end of next and every foll 6th row until there are 97 [101: 105: 113: 119: 125: 133: 139] sts, taking inc sts into patt.

Cont straight until back meas 30 [30: 29: 32: 31: 33: 32: 34] cm, ending with RS facing for next row.

Shape armholes

Keeping patt correct, cast off 3 [4: 4: 5: 5: 6: 6: 7] sts at beg of next 2 rows.

91 [93: 97: 103: 109: 113: 121: 125] sts.

Dec 1 st at each end of next 5 [5: 7: 7: 9: 9: 11:

11] rows, then on foll 4 [4: 3: 4: 4: 4: 4: 5] alt rows. 73 [75: 77: 81: 83: 87: 91: 93] sts.

Cont straight until armhole meas 17 [17: 18: 18: 19: 19: 20: 20] cm, ending with RS facing for next row.

Shape shoulders and back neck

Cast off 6 [6: 7: 7: 7: 8: 9: 9] sts at beg of next 2 rows. 61 [63: 63: 67: 69: 71: 73: 75] sts.

Next row (RS): Cast off 6 [6: 7: 7: 7: 8: 9: 9] sts, patt until there are 9 [10: 9: 11: 11: 11: 11: 12] sts on right needle and turn, leaving rem sts on a holder.

Work each side of neck separately.

Cast off 3 sts at beg of next row.

Cast off rem 6 [7: 6: 8: 8: 8: 8: 9] sts.

With RS facing, rejoin yarn to rem sts, cast off centre 31 [31: 31: 31: 33: 33: 33: 33] sts, patt to end.

Complete to match first side, reversing shapings.

LEFT FRONT

Using 3¾mm (US 5) needles cast on 28 [30: 32: 36: 39: 42: 46: 49] sts.

Beg and ending rows as indicated and repeating the 14 row patt repeat throughout, cont in patt from chart as folls:

Inc 1 st at beg of 2nd row and at same edge on foll 13 rows, then on foll 2 alt rows, then on foll 4th row, taking inc sts into patt, **and at same time**

dec 1 st at beg of 3rd and 4 foll 4th rows. 40 [42: 44: 48: 51: 54: 58: 61] sts.

Work 7 rows, ending with RS facing for next row.

Inc 1 st at beg of next and every foll 6th row until there are 47 [49: 51: 55: 58: 61: 65: 68] sts, taking inc sts into patt.

Cont straight until 2 **patt** rows less have been worked than on back to beg of armhole shaping, ending with RS facing for next row. (**Note:** When comparing lengths/rows, do **NOT** include the first 8 rows of moss st on back – match cast-on edge of front to **top** of these 8 rows.)

Shape front slope

Keeping patt correct, dec 1 st at end of next row.

46 [48: 50: 54: 57: 60: 64: 67] sts.

Work 1 row, ending with RS facing for next row.

Shape armhole

Keeping patt correct, cast off 3 [4: 4: 5: 5: 6: 6: 7] sts at beg and dec 1 st at end of next row.

42 [43: 45: 48: 51: 53: 57: 59] sts.

Work 1 row.

Dec 1 st at armhole edge of next 5 [5: 7: 7: 9: 9: 11: 11] rows, then on foll 4 [4: 3: 4: 4: 4: 4: 5] alt rows **and at same time** dec 1 st at front slope edge of next and foll 6 [6: 6: 6: 7: 7: 6: 6] alt rows, then on 0 [0: 0: 0: 0: 0: 1: 2] foll 4th rows. 26 [27: 28: 30: 30: 32: 34: 34] sts.

Dec 1 st at front slope edge **only** on 2nd [2nd: 2nd: 2nd: 2nd: 2nd: 2nd: 4th] and foll 1 [1: 0: 0:

0: 0: 0: 0] alt rows, then on every foll 4th row until 18 [19: 20: 22: 22: 24: 26: 27] sts rem. Cont straight until left front matches back to beg of shoulder shaping, ending with RS facing for next row.

Shape shoulder

Cast off 6 [6: 7: 7: 7: 8: 9: 9] sts at beg of next and foll alt row.

Work 1 row.

Cast off rem 6 [7: 6: 8: 8: 8: 8: 9] sts.

RIGHT FRONT

Using 3³/4mm (US 5) needles cast on 28 [30: 32: 36: 39: 42: 46: 49] sts.

Beg and ending rows as indicated and repeating the 14 row patt repeat throughout, cont in patt from chart as folls:

Inc 1 st at end of 2nd row and at same edge on foll 13 rows, then on foll 2 alt rows, then on foll 4th row, taking inc sts into patt, **and at same time** dec 1 st at end of 3rd and 4 foll 4th rows.

40 [42: 44: 48: 51: 54: 58: 61] sts.

Complete to match left front, reversing shapings.

SLEEVES

Using 3¹/4mm (US 3) needles cast on 45 [45: 47: 47: 49: 49: 51: 51] sts.

Row 1 (RS): K1, *P1, K1, rep from * to end.

Row 2: As row 1.

These 2 rows form moss st.

Work in moss st for a further 6 rows, ending with RS facing for next row.

Change to 3³/4mm (US 5) needles.

Beg with a K row, work in st st, shaping sides by inc 1 st at each end of 5th [5th: 5th: 3rd: 5th: 3rd: 3rd: 3rd] and every foll 6th [6th: 6th: 6th: 6th: 4th: 4th: 4th] row to 71 [79: 79: 85: 85: 53: 59: 65] sts, then on every foll 8th [8th: 8th: -: 8th: 6th: 6th: 6th] row until there are 79 [81: 83: -: 87: 89: 91: 93] sts.

Cont straight until sleeve meas 44 [44: 45: 45: 46: 46: 45: 45] cm, ending with RS facing for next row.

Shape top

Cast off 3 [4: 4: 5: 5: 6: 6: 7] sts at beg of next 2 rows. 73 [73: 75: 75: 77: 77: 79: 79] sts.

Dec 1 st at each end of next 5 rows, then on every foll alt row to 49 sts, then on foll 9 rows, ending with RS facing for next row. 31 sts.

Cast off 5 sts at beg of next 2 rows.

Cast off rem 21 sts.

MAKING UP

Press as described on the information page.

Join both shoulder seams using back stitch, or mattress stitch if preferred. Join side seams, matching cast-on edge of fronts to top of first 8 rows of moss st on back.

Left front band and collar

With RS facing and using 3¹/4mm (US 3) needles, pick up and knit 7 sts along row-end edge of first 8 rows of back at base of left side seam edge – these are the 8 rows left free below left front cast-on edge.

Work in moss st as given for sleeves until band,

when slightly stretched, fits across cast-on edge of left front to first inc, ending with **WS** facing for next row.

Slip stitch this section of band in place.

**Next row (WS): Moss st 4 sts, wrap next st (by slipping next st from left needle onto right needle, taking yarn to opposite side of work between needles and then slipping same st back onto left needle) and turn.

Next row: Moss st to end.

Work 4 rows across all sts.

Rep from ** 4 times more.

Cont in moss st until band, when slightly stretched, fits up left front opening edge to beg of front slope shaping, ending with RS facing for next row.

Slip stitch this section of band in place, ensuring first section sits neatly around shaped inc row-end edge of front.

Shape for collar

Inc 1 st at beg of next and every foll alt row until there are 31 sts.

Work 4 rows, ending at outer (straight) edge.

***Next row (WS): Moss st 25 sts, wrap next st and turn.

Next row: Moss st to end.

Work 4 rows across all sts.

Rep from *** until shorter (shaped) row-end edge of collar section, unstretched, fits up left front slope and across to centre back neck.

Cast off in moss st.

Slip st in place.

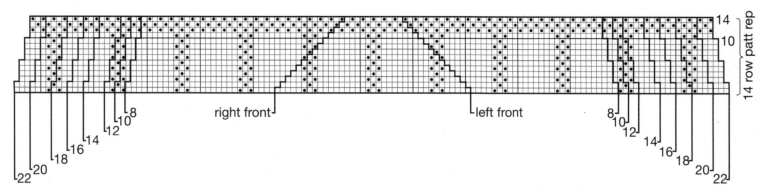

right front   left front

14
10
14 row patt rep

8
10
12
14
16
18
20
22

8
10
12
14
16
18
20
22

key
☐ K on RS, P on WS
⊡ P on RS, K on WS

47

Mark positions for 3 buttons on this band – first to come 2 cm up from last front opening edge inc, last to come 2 cm below beg of front slope shaping and rem button evenly spaced between.

Right front band and collar

Work to match left front band and collar, picking up sts along row-end edge of first 8 rows of back at base of right side seam edge and with the addition of 3 buttonholes worked to correspond with positions marked for buttons as folls:

Buttonhole row (RS): K1, P1, K1, yfwd, K2tog, P1, K1.

When band and collar are complete, cast off.

Slip st in place, joining cast-off edges at centre back neck.

See information page for finishing instructions, setting in sleeves using the set-in method.

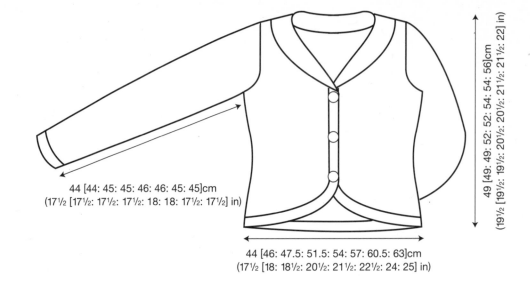

44 [44: 45: 45: 46: 46: 45: 45]cm
(17½ [17½: 17½: 17½: 18: 18: 17½: 17½] in)

49 [49: 49: 52: 52: 54: 54: 56]cm
(19½ [19½: 19½: 20½: 20½: 21½: 21½: 22] in)

44 [46: 47.5: 51.5: 54: 57: 60.5: 63]cm
(17½ [18: 18½: 20½: 21½: 22½: 24: 25] in)

buttercup

main image page 16

SIZE

3-4	5-6	7-8	9-10	11-12	years

To fit chest size

55-57	59-61	63-67	69-73	75-79	cm
21.5-22.5	23-24	25-26.5	27-28.75	29.5-31	in

YARN

Rowan Purelife Organic Cotton

5	6	6	7	8	x 50gm

(photographed in Brazilwood 982)

NEEDLES

1 pair 3¼mm (no 10) (US 3) needles
1 pair 3¾mm (no 9) (US 5) needles
3½mm (no 9) (US E4) crochet hook

TENSION

22 sts and 30 rows to 10 cm measured over st st using 3¾mm (US 5) needles.

BACK

Using 3¼mm (US 3) needles cast on 71 [75: 79: 83: 89] sts.

Work in g st for 8 rows, ending with RS facing for next row.

Change to 3¾mm (US 5) needles.

Beg with a K row, work in st st until back meas 15 [16: 17: 18: 19] cm, ending with RS facing for next row.

Change to 3¾mm (US 5) needles.

Cont in g st until back meas 21 [22: 23: 24: 25] cm, ending with RS facing for next row.

Shape armholes

Cast off 3 sts at beg of next 2 rows.

65 [69: 73: 77: 83] sts.

Dec 1 st at each end of next 3 [3: 3: 1: 1] rows, then on foll 4 [3: 2: 2: 2] alt rows. 51 [57: 63: 71: 77] sts.

Cont straight until armhole meas 14 [15: 16: 17: 18] cm, ending with RS facing for next row.

Shape shoulders and back neck

Cast off 3 [4: 5: 6: 7] sts at beg of next 2 rows.

45 [49: 53: 59: 63] sts.

Next row (RS): Cast off 3 [4: 5: 6: 7] sts, K until there are 7 [7: 7: 8: 9] sts on right needle and turn, leaving rem sts on a holder.

Work each side of neck separately.
Cast off 3 sts at beg of next row.
Cast off rem 4 [4: 4: 5: 6] sts.
With RS facing, rejoin yarn to rem sts, cast off centre 25 [27: 29: 31: 31] sts, K to end.
Complete to match first side, reversing shapings.

FRONT

Work as given for back until 20 [20: 20: 22: 22] rows less have been worked than on back to beg of shoulder shaping, ending with RS facing for next row.

Shape neck

Next row (RS): K21 [23: 25: 29: 32] and turn, leaving rem sts on a holder.
Work each side of neck separately.
Dec 1 st at neck edge of next 8 rows, then on foll 2 [2: 2: 3: 3] alt rows, then on foll 4th row.
10 [12: 14: 17: 20] sts.
Work 3 rows, ending with RS facing for next row.

Shape shoulder

Cast off 3 [4: 5: 6: 7] sts at beg of next and foll alt row.
Work 1 row.
Cast off rem 4 [4: 4: 5: 6] sts.
With RS facing, rejoin yarn to rem sts, cast off centre 9 [11: 13: 13: 13] sts, K to end.
Complete to match first side, reversing shapings.

SLEEVES

Using 3¼mm (US 3) needles cast on 37 [39: 41: 45: 47] sts.
Work in g st for 8 rows, ending with RS facing for next row.
Change to 3¾mm (US 5) needles.
Beg with a K row, work in st st, shaping sides by inc 1 st at each end of 3rd [3rd: 5th: 5th: 7th] and every foll 4th [4th: 6th: 6th: 8th] row to 55 [45: 65: 53: 71] sts, then on every foll 6th [6th: -: 8th: -] row until there are 59 [61: -: 67: -] sts.
Work 3 [3: 3: 7: 1] rows, ending with RS facing for next row.
Change to 3¼mm (US 3) needles.
Work in g st, inc 1 st at each end of 3rd [3rd: 3rd: next: 7th] and every foll 6th [6th: 6th: 8th: 10th] row until there are 65 [67: 69: 71: 75] sts.
Work 1 [1: 7: 7: 1] rows, ending with RS facing for next row.
Change to 3¾mm (US 5) needles.
Beg with a K row, inc 1 st at each end of 5th [5th: next: next: 9th] and foll 6th [6th: 8th: 8th: 0] row. 69 [71: 73: 75: 77] sts.
Cont straight until sleeve meas 31 [35: 39: 43: 47] cm, ending with RS facing for next row.

Shape top

Cast off 4 sts at beg of next 12 rows.
Cast off rem 21 [23: 25: 27: 29] sts.

MAKING UP

Press as described on the information page.
Join right shoulder seam using back stitch, or mattress stitch if preferred.

Neckband

With RS facing and using 3¼mm (US 3) needles, pick up and knit 15 [15: 15: 17: 17] sts down left side of neck, 9 [11: 13: 13: 13] sts from front, 15 [15: 15: 17: 17] sts up right side of neck, then 31 [33: 35: 37: 37] sts from back. 70 [74: 78: 84: 84] sts.
Work in g st for 6 rows, ending with **WS** facing for next row.
Cast off knitwise (on **WS**).
See information page for finishing instructions, setting in sleeves using the shallow set-in method.

Decoration

Using photograph as a guide and 3½mm (US E4) crochet hook, make lengths of chain and sew onto garment to form flowers and curls.

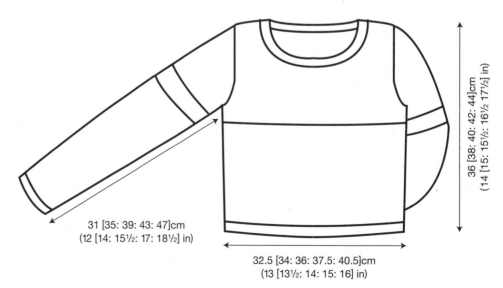

31 [35: 39: 43: 47]cm
(12 [14: 15½: 17: 18½] in)

32.5 [34: 36: 37.5: 40.5]cm
(13 [13½: 14: 15: 16] in)

36 [38: 40: 42: 44]cm
(14 [15: 15½: 16½: 17½] in)

love in a mist 🍃🍃

main image page 10

SIZE

8	10	12	14	16	18	20	22	

To fit bust

81	86	91	97	102	107	112	117	in
32	34	36	38	40	42	44	46	cm

YARN

Rowan Purelife Organic Cotton

9	9	10	10	11	11	12	12	x 50gm

Small amounts of same yarn in 2 contrast colours for embroidery

(photographed in Brazilwood 982, with Madder 980 and Natural 986 used for embroidery)

NEEDLES

1 pair 3¼mm (no 10) (US 3) needles
1 pair 3¾mm (no 9) (US 5) needles
3¼mm (no 10) (US 3) circular needle

BUTTONS

3 x 00417

TENSION

22 sts and 30 rows to 10 cm measured over st st using 3¾mm (US 5) needles.

BACK

Using 3¼mm (US 3) needles cast on 98 [101: 104: 113: 119: 125: 134: 140] sts.

Row 1 (RS): K2, *P1, K2, rep from * to end.

Row 2: P2, *K1, P2, rep from * to end.

These 2 rows form rib.

Work in rib for a further 30 rows, dec [-: inc: -: -: -: dec: dec] 1 st at end of last row and ending with RS facing for next row.

97 [101: 105: 113: 119: 125: 133: 139] sts.

Change to 3¾mm (US 5) needles.

Beg with a K row, work in st st for 70 [70: 66: 76: 72: 78: 76: 82] rows, ending with RS facing for next row. (Back should meas 33 [33: 32: 35: 34: 36: 35: 37] cm.)

Shape armholes

Cast off 3 [4: 4: 5: 5: 6: 6: 7] sts at beg of next 2 rows.

91 [93: 97: 103: 109: 113: 121: 125] sts.

Next row (RS): K2, K2tog, K to last 4 sts, K2tog tbl, K2.

Next row: P2, P2tog tbl, P to last 4 sts, P2tog, P2.

Working all armhole decreases as set by last 2 rows, dec 1 st at each end of next 3 [3: 5: 5: 7: 7: 9: 9] rows, then on foll 4 [4: 3: 4: 4: 4: 4: 5] alt rows.

73 [75: 77: 81: 83: 87: 91: 93] sts.

Cont straight until armhole meas 16 [16: 17: 17: 18: 18: 19: 19] cm, ending with RS facing for next row.

Shape back neck

Next row (RS): K22 [23: 24: 26: 26: 28: 30: 31] and turn, leaving rem sts on a holder.

Work each side of neck separately.

Dec 1 st at neck edge of next row. 21 [22: 23: 25: 25: 27: 29: 30] sts.

Shape shoulder

Cast off 6 [6: 7: 7: 7: 8: 9: 9] sts at beg of next and foll alt row **and at same time** dec 1 st at neck edge of every row.

Work 1 row.

Cast off rem 6 [7: 6: 8: 8: 8: 8: 9] sts.

With RS facing, rejoin yarn to rem sts, cast off centre 29 [29: 29: 29: 31: 31: 31: 31] sts, K to end.

Complete to match first side, reversing shapings.

LEFT FRONT

Using 3¼mm (US 3) needles cast on 48 [51: 51: 57: 60: 63: 66: 69] sts.

Row 1 (RS): *K2, P1, rep from * to end.

Row 2: *K1, P2, rep from * to end.

These 2 rows form rib.

Work in rib for a further 30 rows, – [dec: inc: dec: dec: dec: -: -] 1 st at end of last row and ending with RS facing for next row. 48 [50: 52: 56: 59: 62: 66: 69] sts.

Change to 3¾mm (US 5) needles.

Beg with a K row, work in st st for 12 rows, ending with RS facing for next row.

Shape front slope

Dec 1 st at end of next and 2 [2: 2: 10: 1: 10: 10: 11] foll 4th [4th: 4th: 6th: 4th: 6th: 6th: 6th] rows, then on 8 [8: 7: 0: 9: 0: 0: 0] foll 6th rows.

37 [39: 42: 45: 48: 51: 55: 57] sts.

Work 1 [1: 3: 3: 1: 5: 3: 3] rows, ending with RS facing for next row. (Left front should now match back to beg of armhole shaping.)

Shape armhole

Cast off 3 [4: 4: 5: 5: 6: 6: 7] sts at beg and dec 0 [0: 0: 0: 0: 1: 0: 0] st at end of next row.

34 [35: 38: 40: 43: 44: 49: 50] sts.

Work 1 row.

Working all armhole decreases as set by back, dec 1 st at armhole edge of next 5 [5: 7: 7: 9: 9: 11: 11] rows, then on foll 4 [4: 3: 4: 4: 4: 4: 5] alt rows **and at same time** dec 1 st at front slope edge on 3rd [3rd: next: next: 3rd: 5th: next: next] and every foll 6th [6th: 6th: 6th: 6th: 6th: 6th: 8th] row.

23 [24: 25: 26: 27: 28: 30: 31] sts.

Dec 1 st at front slope edge **only** on 2nd [2nd: 6th: 4th: 4th: 6th: 6th: 4th] and 4 [4: 4: 3: 4: 1: 3: 3] foll 6th [6th: 6th: 8th: 6th: 8th: 6th: 8th] rows, then on 0 [0: 0: 0: 0: 2: 0: 0] foll 8th rows.

18 [19: 20: 22: 22: 24: 26: 27] sts.

Cont straight until left front matches back to beg of shoulder shaping, ending with RS facing for next row.

Shape shoulder

Cast off 6 [6: 7: 7: 7: 8: 9: 9] sts at beg of next and foll alt row.

Work 1 row.

Cast off rem 6 [7: 6: 8: 8: 8: 8: 9] sts.

RIGHT FRONT

Using 3¼mm (US 3) needles cast on 48 [51: 51: 57: 60: 63: 66: 69] sts.

Row 1 (RS): *P1, K2, rep from * to end.

Row 2: *P2, K1, rep from * to end.

These 2 rows form rib.

Work in rib for a further 30 rows, – [dec: inc: dec: dec: dec: -: -] 1 st at beg of last row and ending with RS facing for next row. 48 [50: 52: 56: 59: 62: 66: 69] sts.

Change to 3¾mm (US 5) needles.

Beg with a K row, work in st st for 12 rows, ending with RS facing for next row.

Shape front slope

Dec 1 st at beg of next and 2 [2: 2: 10: 1: 10: 10: 11] foll 4th [4th: 4th: 6th: 4th: 6th: 6th: 6th] rows, then on 8 [8: 7: 0: 9: 0: 0: 0] foll 6th rows.

37 [39: 42: 45: 48: 51: 55: 57] sts.

Complete to match left front, reversing shapings.

SLEEVES

Using 3¼mm (US 3) needles cast on 44 [44: 47: 47: 50: 50: 50: 50] sts.

Work in rib as given for back, inc 1 st at each end of 5th and every foll 8th [6th: 6th: 6th: 6th: 6th: 6th: 6th] row to 54 [54: 55: 59: 62: 62: 62: 62] sts, then on 0 [1: 1: 0: 0: 0: 0: 0] foll 8th row, taking inc sts into rib.

54 [56: 57: 59: 62: 62: 62: 62] sts.

Work 1 [1: 7: 3: 3: 3: 3: 3] rows, inc [inc: -: -: dec: dec: inc: inc] 1 st at centre of last row and ending with RS facing for next row.

55 [57: 57: 59: 61: 61: 63: 63] sts.

Change to 3¾mm (US 5) needles.

Beg with a K row, work in st st, shaping sides by inc 1 st at each end of 7th [7th: next: 3rd: 5th: 3rd: 3rd: 3rd] and every foll 8th [8th: 8th: 6th: 8th: 6th: 6th:

6th] row to 75 [77: 79: 63: 83: 69: 75: 83] sts, then on every foll – [-: -: 8th: -: 8th: 8th: 8th] row until there are – [-: -: 81: -: 85: 87: 89] sts.

Cont straight until sleeve meas 44 [44: 45: 45: 46: 46: 45: 45] cm, ending with RS facing for next row.

Shape top

Cast off 3 [4: 4: 5: 5: 6: 6: 7] sts at beg of next 2 rows.

69 [69: 71: 71: 73: 73: 75: 75] sts.

Working all sleeve top decreases in same way as for armhole decreases, dec 1 st at each end of next 5 rows, then on every foll alt row to 45 sts, then on foll 11 rows, ending with RS facing for next row.

Cast off rem 23 sts.

MAKING UP

Press as described on the information page.

Join both shoulder seams using back stitch, or mattress stitch if preferred.

Front band

With RS facing and using 3¼mm (US 3) circular needle, beg and ending at cast-on edges, pick up and knit 34 sts up right front opening edge to beg of front slope shaping, 97 [97: 97: 104: 104: 110: 110: 115] sts up right front slope to shoulder, 39 [39: 39: 39: 41: 41: 41: 41] sts from back, 97 [97: 97: 104: 104: 110: 110: 115] sts down left front slope to beg of front slope shaping, then 34 sts down left front opening edge 301 [301: 301: 315: 317: 329: 329: 339] sts.

Row 1 (WS): K1, *P1, K1, rep from * to end.

Row 2: K2, P1, K1, *yfwd, K2tog, (P1, K1) 6 times, rep from * once more, yfwd, K2tog, **P1, K1, rep from ** to last st, K1.

Row 3: As row 1.

Row 4: K2, *P1, K1, rep from * to last st, K1.

Row 5: K1, P to last st, K1.

Row 6: Knit.

Rows 7 and 8: As rows 5 and 6.

Row 9: As row 5.

Cast off knitwise.

See information page for finishing instructions, setting in sleeves using the set-in method.

Using photograph as a guide, embroider leaves along front opening edges. Outline leaves and work centre vein in back stitch, then decorate edges with bullion knots.

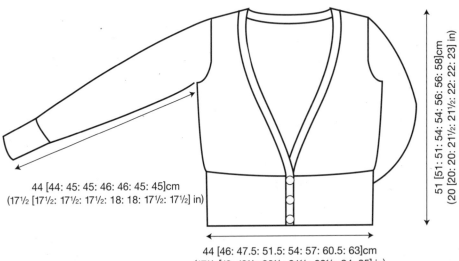

44 [44: 45: 45: 46: 46: 45: 45]cm
(17½ [17½: 17½: 17½: 18: 18: 17½: 17½] in)

44 [46: 47.5: 51.5: 54: 57: 60.5: 63]cm
(17½ [18: 18½: 20½: 21½: 22½: 24: 25] in)

51 [51: 51: 54: 56: 56: 58]cm
(20 [20: 20: 21½: 22: 22: 23] in)

candytuft ❧❧❧

main image page 12

SIZE

3-4	5-6	7-8	9-10	11-12	years
To fit chest size					
55-57	59-61	63-67	69-73	75-79	cm
21.5-22.5	23-24	25-26.5	27-28.75	29.5-31	in

YARN

Rowan Purelife Organic Cotton

7	8	8	9	9	x 50gm

(photographed in 980 Madder)

NEEDLES

3¹/2mm (no 9) (US E4) crochet hook

TENSION

4 patt reps (20 sts) to 9 cm, and 10 rows to 10 cm measured over main patt using 3.50mm (US E4) crochet hook.

UK CROCHET ABBREVIATIONS

ch = chain; **dc** = double crochet; **ss** = slip stitch; **tr** = treble; **dc2tog** = (insert hook as indicated, yarn over hook and draw loop through) twice, yarn over hook and draw through all 3 loops on hook; **tr2tog** = (yarn over hook and insert hook as indicated, yarn over hook and draw loop through, yarn over hook and draw through 2 loops) twice, yarn over hook and draw through all 3 loops on hook.

BODY (worked in one piece to armholes)
Using 3¹/2mm (US E4) crochet hook make 153 [171: 177: 195: 201] ch.
Row 1 (WS): 1 dc into 2nd ch from hook, 1 dc into next ch, *6 ch, miss 4 ch, 1 dc into each of next 2 ch, rep from * to end, turn. 25 [28: 29: 32: 33] patt reps.
Row 2: 3 ch (counts as first tr), miss dc at base of 3 ch, 1 tr into next dc, *2 ch, 1 dc into next ch sp, 2 ch, 1 tr into each of next 2 dc, rep from * to end, turn.
Row 3: 3 ch (counts as first tr), miss tr at base of 3 ch, 1 tr into next tr, *3 ch, miss 1 ch sp, 1 ss into next dc, 3 ch, miss 1 ch sp, 1 tr into each of next 2 tr, rep from * to end, working tr at end of last rep into top of 3 ch at beg of previous row, turn.
Row 4: 1 ch (does NOT count as st), 1 dc into each of first 2 tr, *4 ch, miss (3 ch, 1 ss and 3 ch), 1 dc into each of next 2 tr, rep from * to end, working tr at end of last rep into top of 3 ch at beg of previous row, turn.
Row 5: 1 ch (does NOT count as st), 1 dc into each of first 2 dc, *6 ch, miss 4 ch, 1 dc into each of next 2 dc, rep from * to end, turn.
Rows 6 to 9: As rows 2 to 5.
Row 10: 1 ch (does NOT count as st), 1 dc into each of first 2 dc, *4 dc into next ch sp, 1 dc into each of next 2 dc, rep from * to end, turn.
152 [170: 176: 194: 200] sts.
Row 11: 1 ch (does NOT count as st), 1 dc into each of first 5 [6: 3: 2: 9] dc, dc2tog over next 2 dc, (1 dc into each of next 12 [10: 10: 9: 8] dc, dc2tog over next 2 dc) 10 [13: 14: 17: 18] times, 1 dc into each of last 5 [6: 3: 3: 9] dc, turn. 141 [156: 161: 176: 181] sts.
Row 12: 5 ch (counts as 1 tr and 2 ch), tr2tog into st at base of 5 ch, *miss 4 dc, (tr2tog, 2 ch, tr2tog, 2 ch and tr2tog) into next dc, rep from * to last 5 dc, miss 4 dc, (tr2tog, 2 ch and 1 tr) into last dc, turn.

Now work in main patt as folls:
Row 1 (WS): 1 ch (does NOT count as st), 1 dc into tr at base of 1 ch, *4 ch, miss (2 ch, 2 tr2tog and 2 ch), 1 dc into next tr2tog, rep from * to end, working dc at end of last rep into 3rd of 5 ch at beg of previous row, turn. 28 [31: 32: 35: 36] patt reps.
Row 2: 5 ch (counts as 1 tr and 2 ch), tr2tog into dc at base of 5 ch, *miss 4 ch, (tr2tog, 2 ch, tr2tog, 2 ch and tr2tog) into next dc, rep from * to last 5 dc, miss 4 ch, (tr2tog, 2 ch and 1 tr) into last dc, turn.
These 2 rows form main patt.
Cont in main patt until work meas approx 19 [20: 21: 22: 23] cm, ending with RS facing for next row.
Divide for armholes
Next row (RS): 5 ch (counts as 1 tr and 2 ch), tr2tog into dc at base of 5 ch, *miss 4 ch, (tr2tog, 2 ch, tr2tog, 2 ch and tr2tog) into next dc, rep from * 5 [6: 6: 7: 7] times more, miss 4 ch, 1 tr into next dc and turn, leaving rem sts unworked.
Work on this set of 6¹/2 [7¹/2: 7¹/2: 8¹/2: 8¹/2] patt reps only for right front.
Next row: ss across 1 tr, tr2tog, 2 ch and into next tr2tog, 1 ch (does NOT count as st), 1 dc into tr2tog at base of 1 ch, patt to end, turn. 6 [7: 7: 8: 8] patt reps.
Next row: 5 ch (counts as 1 tr and 2 ch), tr2tog into dc at base of 5 ch, *miss 4 ch, (tr2tog, 2 ch, tr2tog, 2 ch and tr2tog) into next dc, rep from * 4 [5: 5: 6: 6] times more, miss 4 ch, 1 tr into next dc, turn.
Next row: ss across 1 tr, tr2tog, 2 ch and into next tr2tog, 1 ch (does NOT count as st), 1 dc into tr2tog at base of 1 ch, patt to end, turn. 5 [6: 6: 7: 7] patt reps.
Work 6 [6: 8: 8: 10] rows, ending with RS facing for next row.

Shape neck
Next row (RS): ss across 1 dc and 4 ch and into next dc, 3 ch (counts as 1 tr), miss 4 ch, (tr2tog, 2 ch, tr2tog, 2 ch and tr2tog) into next dc, patt to end, turn.
Next row: Patt until dc has been worked into centre tr2tog of last full tr2tog group, turn.
Next row: 3 ch (counts as 1 tr), miss dc at base of 3 ch and 4 ch, (tr2tog, 2 ch, tr2tog, 2 ch and tr2tog) into next dc, patt to end, turn.
Next row: Patt until dc has been worked into centre tr2tog of last full tr2tog group, turn. 2 [3: 3: 4: 4] patt reps.
Rep last 2 rows 0 [1: 0: 1: 1] times more. 2 [2: 3: 3: 3] patt reps.
Work 2 [0: 2: 0: 0] rows.
Fasten off.

Shape back
Return to last complete row worked before dividing for armholes, rejoin yarn to same dc as used for tr at end of first row of right front and cont as folls:
Next row (RS): 3 ch (counts as 1 tr), miss 4 ch, *(tr2tog, 2 ch, tr2tog, 2 ch and tr2tog) into next dc, miss 4 ch, rep from * 12 [13: 14: 15: 16] times more, 1 tr into next dc and turn, leaving rem 7 [8: 8: 9: 9] patt reps unworked.
Next row: ss across 1 tr, tr2tog, 2 ch and into next tr2tog, 1 ch (does NOT count as st), 1 dc into tr2tog at base of 1 ch, patt until dc has been worked into centre tr2tog of last full tr2tog group, turn. 12 [13: 14: 15: 16] patt reps.
Next row: 3 ch (counts as 1 tr), miss dc at base of 3 ch and next 4 ch, (tr2tog, 2 ch, tr2tog, 2 ch and tr2tog) into next dc, patt until (tr2tog, 2 ch, tr2tog, 2 ch and tr2tog) has been worked into last-but-one dc of previous row, miss 4 ch, 1 tr into last dc, turn.

Next row: ss across 1 tr, tr2tog, 2 ch and into next tr2tog, 1 ch (does NOT count as st), 1 dc into tr2tog at base of 1 ch, patt until dc has been worked into centre tr2tog of last full tr2tog group, turn. 10 [11: 12: 13: 14] patt reps.

Work 12 [12: 14: 14: 16] rows, ending with RS facing for next row.

Fasten off, placing markers either side of centre 6 [7: 6: 7: 8] patt reps to denote back neck.

Shape left front

Return to last complete row worked before dividing for armholes, rejoin yarn to same dc as used for tr at end of first row of back and complete to match right front, reversing shapings.

SLEEVES

Using 3½mm (US E4) crochet hook make 51 [51: 51: 51: 57] ch.

Work rows 1 to 10 as given for body. 8 [8: 8: 8: 10] patt reps, 50 [50: 50: 50: 56] sts.

Row 11: 1 ch (does NOT count as st), 1 dc into each of first 4 [4: 4: 4: 5] dc, dc2tog over next 2 dc, (1 dc into each of next 11 [11: 11: 11: 9] dc, dc2tog over next 2 dc) 3 [3: 3: 3: 4] times, 1 dc into each of last 5 dc, turn. 46 [46: 46: 46: 51] sts.

Work row 12 as given for body.

Now work in main patt as given for body for 3 rows, ending with RS facing for next row. 9 [9: 9: 9: 11] patt reps.

Next row (RS): 3 ch (does NOT count as st), (1 tr, 2 ch, tr2tog, 2 ch and tr2tog) into dc at base of 3 ch, *miss 4 ch, (tr2tog, 2 ch, tr2tog, 2 ch and tr2tog) into next dc, rep from * to end, turn.

Next row: 1 ch (does NOT count as st), 1 dc into tr2tog at base of 1 ch, 2 ch, miss 2 ch, 1 dc into next tr2tog, *4 ch, miss (2 ch, 2 tr2tog and 2 ch), 1 dc into next tr2tog, rep from * to last 3 sts, 2 ch, miss 2 ch, 1 dc into next tr, turn.

Next row: 5 ch (counts as 1 tr and 2 ch), tr2tog into dc at base of 3 ch, miss 2 ch, *(tr2tog, 2 ch, tr2tog, 2 ch and tr2tog) into next dc**, miss 4 ch, rep from * to end, ending last rep at **, miss 2 ch, (tr2tog, 2 ch and 1 tr) into last dc, turn. 11 [11: 11: 11: 13] patt reps.

Work 5 [7: 5: 7: 9] rows.

Rep last 8 [10: 8: 10: 12] rows 0 [0: 1: 1: 1] times more, then first 3 of these rows again.
13 [13: 15: 15: 17] patt reps.

Cont straight until sleeve meas approx 28 [32: 36: 40: 44] cm, ending with RS facing for next row.

Shape top

Next row (RS): 3 ch (counts as 1 tr), miss dc at base of 3 ch and next 4 ch, *(tr2tog, 2 ch, tr2tog, 2 ch and tr2tog) into next dc, miss 4 ch, rep from * to last st, 1 tr into last dc, turn.

Next row: ss across 1 tr, tr2tog, 2 ch and into next tr2tog, 1 ch (does NOT count as st), 1 dc into tr2tog at base of 1 ch, patt until dc has been worked into centre tr2tog of last full tr2tog group, turn.
11 [11: 13: 13: 15] patt reps.

Rep last 2 rows once more. 9 [9: 11: 11: 13] patt reps.
Fasten off.

MAKING UP

Press as described on the information page.

Join both shoulder seams using back stitch, or mattress stitch if preferred.

See information page for finishing instructions, setting in sleeves using the shallow set-in method.

Body edging

With RS facing and using 3½mm (US E4) crochet hook, attach yarn at base of left front opening edge, 1 ch (does NOT count as st), work in dc evenly along entire foundation ch edge, ensuring number of dc worked is a multiple of 3 sts plus 2 extra and placing markers on first and last of these dc, work in dc up right front opening edge to beg of neck shaping, work in dc evenly around entire neck edge, ensuring number of dc worked is a multiple of 3 sts plus 2 extra and placing markers on first and last of these dc, then work in dc evenly down left front opening edge, ss to first (marked) dc.

Next round (RS): 1 ch (does NOT count as st), 2 dc into first (marked) dc, 5 tr into next dc, *miss 1 dc, 1 dc into next dc, miss 1 dc, 5 tr into next dc, rep from * until 5 tr have been worked into dc before next marked dc, 2 dc into marked dc, 1 dc into each dc to next marked dc, 1 dc into next marked dc, make a ch approx 20 cm long, 1 dc into 2nd ch from hook, 1 dc into each ch to end, 1 dc into same marked dc, 5 tr into next dc, **miss 1 dc, 1 dc into next dc, miss 1 dc, 5 tr into next dc, rep from ** until 5 tr have been worked into dc before last marked dc, 1 dc into this marked dc, make a ch approx 20 cm long, 1 dc into 2nd ch from hook, 1 dc into each ch to end, 1 dc into same marked dc, 1 dc into each dc to end, ss to first dc.
Fasten off.

Cuff edgings (both alike)

With RS facing and using 3½mm (US E4) crochet hook, attach yarn at base of sleeve seam, 1 ch (does NOT count as st), work in dc evenly around lower edge of sleeve, ensuring number of dc worked is a multiple of 3 sts, ss to first dc.

Next round (RS): 1 ch (does NOT count as st), 1 dc into first dc, *miss 1 dc, 5 tr into next dc, miss 1 dc, 1 dc into next dc, rep from * to end, replacing dc at end of last rep with ss to first dc.
Fasten off.

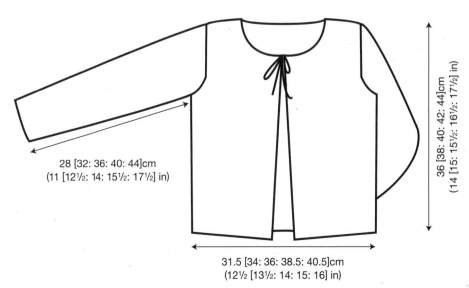

28 [32: 36: 40: 44]cm
(11 [12½: 14: 15½: 17½] in)

36 [38: 40: 42: 44]cm
(14 [15: 15½: 16½: 17½] in)

31.5 [34: 36: 38.5: 40.5]cm
(12½ [13½: 14: 15: 16] in)

moonflower

main image page 14

SIZE

8	10	12	14	16	18	20	22	
To fit bust								
81	86	91	97	102	107	112	117	in
32	34	36	38	40	42	44	46	cm

YARN

Rowan Purelife Organic Cotton

9	9	10	10	11	11	12	12	x 50gm

(photographed in Yellowwood 984)

NEEDLES

1 pair 3¼mm (no 10) (US 3) needles
1 pair 3¾mm (no 9) (US 5) needles
Cable needle

TENSION

22 sts and 30 rows to 10 cm measured over st st
using 3¾mm (US 5) needles.

SPECIAL ABBREVIATIONS

C4B = slip next 2 sts onto cable needle and leave
at back of work, K2, then K2 from cable needle;
C4F = slip next 2 sts onto cable needle and leave
at front of work, K2, then K2 from cable needle;
C7F = slip next 3 sts onto cable needle and leave
at front of work, K4, then K3 from cable needle.

BACK

Using 3¼mm (US 3) needles cast on 94 [98: 102: 106: 114: 122: 126: 134] sts.

Row 1 (RS): K2, *P2, K2, rep from * to end.

Row 2: P2, *K2, P2, rep from * to end.

These 2 rows form rib.

Work in rib for a further 18 rows, dec [dec: dec: inc: inc: dec: inc: inc] 1 st at end of last row and ending with RS facing for next row.

93 [97: 101: 107: 115: 121: 127: 135] sts.

Change to 3¾mm (US 5) needles.**

Beg with a K row, work in st st until back meas 27 [27: 26: 29: 28: 30: 29: 31] cm, ending with RS facing for next row.

Shape raglan armholes

Cast off 3 sts at beg of next 2 rows.

87 [91: 95: 101: 109: 115: 121: 129] sts.

Sizes 8, 10, 12, 14 and 16

Next row (RS): K1, yfwd, K2tog (to make an eyelet), K2tog tbl (to dec 1 st), K to last 5 sts, K2tog (to dec 1 st), K2tog tbl, yfwd (to make an eyelet), K1.

Next row: Purl.

Next row: K1, yfwd, K2tog (to make an eyelet), K to last 3 sts, K2tog tbl, yfwd (to make an eyelet), K1.

Next row: Purl.

Rep last 4 rows 9 [7: 7: 4: 2: -: -: -] times more.

67 [75: 79: 91: 103: -: -: -] sts.

Sizes 20 and 22

Next row (RS): K1, yfwd, K2tog (to make an eyelet), K2tog tbl (to dec 1 st), K to last 5 sts, K2tog (to dec 1 st), K2tog tbl, yfwd (to make an eyelet), K1.

Next row: P3, P2tog, P to last 5 sts, P2tog tbl, P3.

Rep last 2 rows – [-: -: -: -: -: 0: 4] times more.

- [-: -: -: -: -: 117: 109] sts.

All sizes

Next row (RS): K1, yfwd, K2tog (to make an eyelet), K2tog tbl (to dec 1 st), K to last 5 sts, K2tog (to dec 1 st), K2tog tbl, yfwd (to make an eyelet), K1.

Next row: Purl.

Rep last 2 rows 14 [18: 20: 26: 31: 37: 38: 34] times more, ending with RS facing for next row.

Cast off rem 37 [37: 37: 37: 39: 39: 39: 39] sts.

FRONT

Work as given for back to **.

Now work in patt as folls:

Row 1 (RS): K24 [26: 28: 31: 35: 38: 41: 45], P1, K4, P1, K1, (K5, yfwd, sl 1, K1, psso, K3) 3 times, K2, P1, K4, P1, K to end.

Row 2 and every foll alt row: P24 [26: 28: 31: 35: 38: 41: 45], K1, P4, K1, P33, K1, P4, K1, P to end.

Row 3: K24 [26: 28: 31: 35: 38: 41: 45], P1, C4B, P1, K1, (K3, K2tog, yfwd, K1, yfwd, sl 1, K1, psso, K2) 3 times, K2, P1, C4F, P1, K to end.

Row 5: K24 [26: 28: 31: 35: 38: 41: 45], P1, K4, P1, K1, (K2, K2tog, yfwd, K3, yfwd, sl 1, K1, psso, K1) 3 times, K2, P1, K4, P1, K to end.

Row 7: K24 [26: 28: 31: 35: 38: 41: 45], P1, K4, P1, K1, (K1, K2tog, yfwd, K5, yfwd, sl 1, K1, psso) 3 times, K2, P1, K4, P1, K to end.

Row 9: K24 [26: 28: 31: 35: 38: 41: 45], P1, K4, P1, K1, K2tog, yfwd, (K7, yfwd, sl 1, K2tog, psso, yfwd) twice, K7, yfwd, sl 1, K1, psso, K1, P1, K4, P1, K to end.

Row 11: K24 [26: 28: 31: 35: 38: 41: 45], P1, C4B, P1, K1, (C7F, K3) 3 times, K2, P1, C4F, P1, K to end.

Row 12: As row 2.

These 12 rows form patt.

Cont in patt until front matches back to beg of raglan armhole shaping, ending with RS facing for next row.

Shape raglan armholes

Keeping patt correct, cast off 3 sts at beg of next 2 rows. 87 [91: 95: 101: 109: 115: 121: 129] sts.

Making eyelets on every RS row as set by back and working all raglan decreases 3 sts in from ends of rows as set by back, cont as folls:

Dec 1 st at each end of next 1 [1: 1: 1: 1: 1: 3: 11] rows, then on 10 [8: 8: 5: 3: 0: 0: 0] foll 4th rows, then on every foll alt row until 57 [57: 57: 59: 61: 61: 63: 63] sts rem.

Work 1 row, ending with RS facing for next row.

Shape neck

Next row (RS): K1, yfwd, K2tog (for eyelet), K2tog tbl (for dec), patt 11 [11: 11: 13: 13: 13: 15: 15] sts and turn, leaving rem sts on a holder.

Work each side of neck separately.

Keeping patt correct, dec 1 st at neck edge of next 6 rows, then on foll 0 [0: 0: 1: 1: 1: 2: 2] alt rows and at same time dec 1 st at raglan armhole edge on 2nd and every foll alt row. 6 sts.

Work 1 row, ending with RS facing for next row.

Next row (RS): K1, yfwd, K2tog, sl 1, K2tog, psso.

Next row: P4.

Next row: K1, sl 1, K2tog, psso.

Next row: P2.

Next row: K2tog and fasten off.

With RS facing, rejoin yarn to rem sts, cast off centre 25 [25: 25: 23: 25: 25: 23: 23] sts, patt to last 5 sts, K2tog (to dec 1 st), K2tog tbl, yfwd (to make an eyelet), K1.

Complete to match first side, reversing shapings.

SLEEVES

Using 3¼mm (US 3) needles cast on 46 [46: 46: 46: 50: 50: 50: 50] sts.

Work in rib as given for back for 20 rows, dec [dec: inc: inc: dec: dec: inc: inc] 1 st at end of last row and ending with RS facing for next row.

45 [45: 47: 47: 49: 49: 51: 51] sts.

Change to 3¾mm (US 5) needles.

Beg with a K row, work in st st, shaping sides by inc 1 st at each end of 3rd and every foll 4th row to 71 [71: 77: 77: 75: 75: 87: 87] sts, then on every foll 6th row until there are 87 [87: 91: 91: 93: 93: 97: 97] sts.

Cont straight until sleeve meas 44 [44: 45: 45: 46: 46: 45: 45] cm, ending with RS facing for next row.

Shape raglan

Cast off 3 sts at beg of next 2 rows.

81 [81: 85: 85: 87: 87: 91: 91] sts.

Making eyelets on every RS row as set by back and working all raglan decreases 3 sts in from ends of rows as set by back, cont as folls:

Dec 1 st at each end of next and 5 foll 4th rows, then on every foll alt row to 29 sts.

Work 1 row, ending with RS facing for next row.

Keeping eyelets and decreases correct as set, cont as folls:

Left sleeve only

Dec 1 st at each end of next row, then cast off 4 sts at beg of foll row. 23 sts.

Dec 1 st at beg of next row, then cast off 5 sts at beg of foll row. 17 sts.

Rep last 2 rows twice more.

Right sleeve only

Cast off 5 sts at beg and dec 1 st at end of next row. 23 sts.

Work 1 row.

Rep last 2 rows 3 times more.

Both sleeves

Cast off rem 5 sts.

MAKING UP

Press as described on the information page.

Join both front and right back raglan seams using back stitch, or mattress stitch if preferred.

Neckband

With RS facing and using 3¼mm (US 3) needles, pick up and knit 21 sts from top of left sleeve, 12 [12: 12: 14: 14: 14: 16: 16] sts down left side of neck, 25 [25: 25: 23: 25: 25: 23: 23] sts from front, 12 [12: 12: 14: 14: 14: 16: 16] sts up right side of neck, 21 sts from top of right sleeve, then 36 [36: 36: 36: 38: 38: 38: 38] sts from back.

127 [127: 127: 129: 133: 133: 135: 135] sts.

Row 1 (WS): P1, *K1, P1, rep from * to end.

Row 2: K1, *P1, K1, rep from * to end.

Rep these 2 rows twice more, ending with **WS** facing for next row.

Cast off in rib (on **WS**).

See information page for finishing instructions.

44 [44: 45: 45: 46: 46: 45: 45]cm
(17½ [17½: 17½: 17½: 18: 18: 17½: 17½] in)

42.5 [44: 46: 48.5: 52.5: 55: 57.5: 61.5]cm
(16½ [17½: 18: 19: 20½: 21½: 22½: 24] in)

56 [56: 56: 59: 59: 61: 61: 63]cm
(22 [22: 22: 23: 23: 24: 24: 25] in)

carnation

main image page 18

SIZE

	3-4	5-6	7-8	9-10	11-12	years

To fit chest size

	55-57	59-61	63-67	69-73	75-79	cm
	21.5-22.5	23-24	25-26.5	27-28.75	29.5-31	in

YARN

Rowan Purelife Organic Cotton

	5	5	5	6	6	x 50gm

(photographed in Natural 986)

NEEDLES

1 pair 3¹/4mm (no 10) (US 3) needles
1 pair 3³/4mm (no 9) (US 5) needles

TENSION

20 sts and 32 rows to 10 cm measured over patt using 3³/4mm (US 5) needles.

BACK

Using 3³/4mm (US 5) needles cast on 83 [87: 93: 95: 99] sts.

Row 1 (RS): K1, *P1, K1, rep from * to end.

Row 2: P1, *K1, P1, rep from * to end.

These 2 rows form rib.

Work in rib for a further 2 rows, ending with RS facing for next row.

Row 5 (RS): rib 2 [4: 3: 4: 6], work 2 tog, (rib 9 [9: 10: 10: 10], work 2 tog) 7 times, rib to end.

75 [79: 85: 87: 91] sts.

Now work in patt as folls:

Row 1 (WS): K0 [2: 2: 0: 2], P3, *K3, P3, rep from * to last 0 [2: 2: 0: 2] sts, K0 [2: 2: 0: 2].

Row 2: (K2tog, yfrn) 0 [1: 1: 0: 1] times, P3, *yon, K3tog, yfrn, P3, rep from * to last 0 [2: 2: 0: 2] sts, (yon, K2tog) 0 [1: 1: 0: 1] times.

Row 3: P0 [2: 2: 0: 2], K3, *P3, K3, rep from * to last 0 [2: 2: 0: 2] sts, P0 [2: 2: 0: 2].

Row 4: (K1, K2tog, yfrn) 1 [0: 0: 1: 0] times, P3 [2: 2: 3: 2], *yon, K3tog, yfrn, P3, rep from * to last 3 [5: 5: 3: 5] sts, (yon, K2tog, K1) 1 [0: 0: 1: 0] times, (yon, K3tog, yfrn, P2) 0 [1: 1: 0: 1] times.

These 4 rows form patt.

Cont straight until back meas 10 [11: 12: 13: 14] cm, ending with RS facing for next row.

Keeping patt correct, dec 1 st at each end of next and every foll 20th row until 63 [67: 73: 75: 79] sts rem.

Cont straight until back meas 50 [51: 52: 53: 54] cm, ending with RS facing for next row.

Shape armholes

Keeping patt correct, cast off 3 sts at beg of next 2 rows. 57 [61: 67: 69: 73] sts.

Dec 1 st at each end of next 5 [5: 5: 3: 3] rows, then on foll 3 [2: 2: 2: 1] alt rows. 41 [47: 53: 59: 65] sts.

Cont straight until armhole meas 12 [13: 14: 15: 16] cm, ending with RS facing for next row.

Shape back neck

Next row (RS): Patt 10 [12: 14: 16: 19] sts and turn, leaving rem sts on a holder.

Work each side of neck separately.

Keeping patt correct, dec 1 st at neck edge of next 3 rows, ending with RS facing for next row.

7 [9: 11: 13: 16] sts.

Shape shoulder

Cast off 3 [4: 5: 6: 7] sts at beg and dec 1 st at end of next row.

Work 1 row.

Cast off rem 3 [4: 5: 6: 8] sts.

With RS facing, rejoin yarn to rem sts, cast off centre 21 23: 25: 27: 27] sts, patt to end.

Complete to match first side, reversing shapings.

FRONT

Work as given for back until 24 [24: 24: 26: 26] rows less have been worked than on back to beg of shoulder shaping, ending with RS facing for next row.

Shape neck

Next row (RS): Patt 16 [18: 20: 23: 26] sts and turn, leaving rem sts on a holder.

Work each side of neck separately.

Keeping patt correct, dec 1 st at neck edge of next 6 rows, then on foll 2 [2: 2: 3: 3] alt rows, then on 2 foll 4th rows. 6 [8: 10: 12: 15] sts.

Work 5 rows, ending with RS facing for next row.

Shape shoulder

Cast off 3 [4: 5: 6: 7] sts at beg of next row.

Work 1 row.

Cast off rem 3 [4: 5: 6: 8] sts.

With RS facing, rejoin yarn to rem sts, cast off centre 9 [11: 13: 13: 13] sts, patt to end.

Complete to match first side, reversing shapings.

MAKING UP

Press as described on the information page.

Join right shoulder seam using back stitch, or mattress stitch if preferred.

Neckband

With RS facing and using 3¹/4mm (US 3) needles, pick up and knit 24 [24: 24: 26: 26] sts down left side of neck, 9 [11: 13: 13: 13] sts from front, 24 [24: 24: 26: 26] sts up right side of neck, then 32 [34: 36: 38: 38] sts from back. 89 [93: 97: 103: 103] sts.

Work in rib as given for back for 4 rows, ending with **WS** facing for next row.

Cast off in rib (on **WS**).

Join left shoulder and neckband seam.

Armhole borders (both alike)

With RS facing and using 3¹/4mm (US 3) needles, pick up and knit 67 [71: 77: 81: 85] sts evenly all round armhole edge.

Work in rib as given for back for 4 rows, ending with **WS** facing for next row.
Cast off in rib (on **WS**).

Pockets (both alike)

Using 3¾mm (US 5) needles cast on 19 sts.

Row 1 (RS): K2tog, yfrn, P3, *yon, K3tog, yfrn, P3, rep from * to last 2 sts, yon, K2tog.

Row 2: P2, K3, *P3, K3, rep from * to last 2 sts, P2.

Row 3: P2, *yon, K3tog, yfrn, P3, rep from * to last 5 sts, yon, K3tog, yfrn, P2.

Row 4: K2, P3, *K3, P3, rep from * to last 2 sts, K2.
These 4 rows form patt.

Work in patt for a further 24 rows, inc 1 st at each end of last row and ending with RS facing for next row.
21 sts.

Beg with row 2, work in rib as given for back for 4 rows, ending with RS facing for next row.
Cast off in rib.

See information page for finishing instructions. Using photograph as a guide, sew pockets onto front.

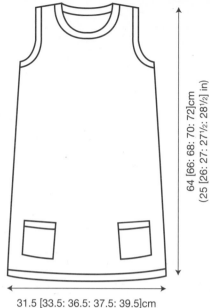

cherry pie

main image page 22

SIZE

3-4	5-6	7-8	9-10	11-12	years

To fit chest size

55-57	59-61	63-67	69-73	75-79	cm
21.5-22.5	23-24	25-26.5	27-28.75	29.5-31	in

YARN

Rowan Purelife Organic Cotton

6	6	7	8	8	x 50gm

(photographed in Yellowwood 984)

NEEDLES

1 pair 3¾mm (no 9) (US 5) needles
3½mm (no 9) (US E4) crochet hook

TENSION

22 sts and 30 rows to 10 cm measured over st st using 3¾mm (US 5) needles.

UK CROCHET ABBREVIATIONS

ch = chain; **dc** = double crochet; **ss** = slip stitch; **tr** = treble.

BACK

Using 3¾mm (US 5) needles cast on 93 [97: 101: 105: 111] sts.

Beg with a K row, work in st st until back meas 20 [22: 24: 26: 28] cm, ending with RS facing for next row.

Shape back neck

Next row (RS): K8 [10: 12: 13: 16], K2tog, (K2, K2tog) 19 times, K1 [1: 1: 10: 10] and slip these 67 [69: 71: 81: 84] sts onto a holder, K to end.
Work each side of neck separately.
Cont straight on these 6 [8: 10: 4: 7] sts for a further 14 cm, ending with RS facing for next row.

Shape shoulder

Cast off.
With **WS** facing, rejoin yarn to rem sts, cast off centre 61 [61: 61: 77: 77] sts, P to end.
Complete to match first side.

FRONT

Using 3¾mm (US 5) needles cast on 93 [97: 101: 105: 111] sts.

Beg with a K row, work in st st until front meas 13 [15: 17: 19: 21] cm, ending with RS facing for next row.

Shape front neck

Next row (RS): K8 [10: 12: 13: 16], K2tog, (K2, K2tog) 19 times, K1 [1: 1: 10: 10] and slip these 67 [69: 71: 81: 84] sts onto a holder, K to end.

Work each side of neck separately.
Cont straight on these 6 [8: 10: 4: 7] sts for a further 21 cm, ending with RS facing for next row.

Shape shoulder
Cast off.
With **WS** facing, rejoin yarn to rem sts, cast off centre 61 [61: 61: 77: 77] sts, P to end.
Complete to match first side.

SLEEVES

Using 3³⁄₄mm (US 5) needles cast on 47 [47: 61: 61: 61] sts.
Beg with a K row, work in st st, shaping sides by inc 1 st at each end of 3rd [3rd: 9th: 7th: 7th] and every foll 4th [4th: 10th: 8th: 8th] row to 53 [59: 75: 69: 77] sts, then on every foll 6th [6th: -: 10th: 10th] row until there are 65 [71: -: 79: 83] sts.
Cont straight until sleeve meas 20 [24: 28: 32: 36] cm, ending with RS facing for next row.
Cast off.

MAKING UP

Press as described on the information page.
Join both shoulder seams using back stitch, or mattress stitch if preferred. Place markers along side seam edges 15 [16: 17: 18: 19] cm down from shoulder seams to denote base of armholes.
See information page for finishing instructions, setting in sleeves using the straight cast-off method.

Basic motif
Using 3¹⁄₂mm (US E4) crochet hook make 6 ch and join with a ss to form a ring.
Round 1 (RS): 3 ch (counts as first tr), 15 tr into ring, ss to top of 3 ch at beg of round.
Round 2: 3 ch (counts as first tr), 2 tr into st at base of 3 ch, *2 ch, miss 1 tr, 1 tr into next tr, 2 ch, miss 1 tr**, 3 tr into next tr, rep from * to end, ending last rep at **, ss to top of 3 ch at beg of round.
Round 3: 3 ch (counts as first tr), miss st at base of 3 ch, *5 tr into next tr, (1 tr into next tr, 2 ch, miss 2 ch) twice**, 1 tr into next tr, rep from * to end, ending last rep at **, ss to top of 3 ch at beg of round.
Fasten off.
Basic motif is a square – in each corner there are 5 tr and along sides between these 5 tr are a further 7 sts.

Hemband
Make 11 [11: 12: 12: 13] basic motifs and join to form a loop. Slip stitch loop to lower cast-on edge of back and front, easing in slight fullness.

Cuffs (both alike)
Make 3 [3: 4: 4: 4] basic motifs and join to form a loop. Slip stitch loop to lower cast-on edge of sleeve.

Neckband
Make 14 [14: 14: 16: 16] basic motifs and join to form shape shown in diagram. Slip stitch in place to back and front neck edges, gathering in fullness to fit edges of motifs.

Hem edging
With RS facing and 3¹⁄₂mm (US E4) crochet hook, attach yarn to lower edge of hemband, 1 ch (does NOT count as st), work 1 round of dc evenly around entire lower edge, ending with ss to first dc.
Next round: 1 ch (does NOT count as st), 1 dc into each dc to end, ss to first dc.
Rep last round once more.
Fasten off.

Cuff edging
Work around lower edge of cuffs as given for hem edging.

Neck edging
Work around entire neck opening edge as given for hem edging, missing dc as required at either side of neck corner points to shape corners of edging and ensure it lays flat.

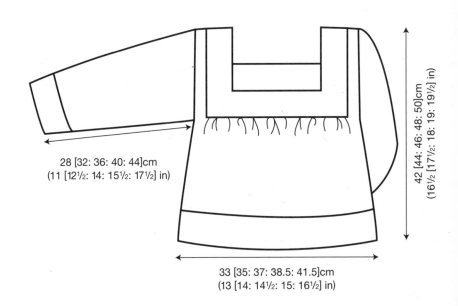

28 [32: 36: 40: 44]cm
(11 [12¹⁄₂: 14: 15¹⁄₂: 17¹⁄₂] in)

42 [44: 46: 48: 50]cm
(16¹⁄₂ [17¹⁄₂: 18: 19: 19¹⁄₂] in)

33 [35: 37: 38.5: 41.5]cm
(13 [14: 14¹⁄₂: 15: 16¹⁄₂] in)

woodruff

main image page 25

SIZE

	S	M	L	XL	
To fit bust					
	81-86	91-97	102-107	112-117	cm
	32-34	36-38	40-42	44-46	in

YARN

Rowan Purelife Organic Cotton

	9	10	11	13	x 50gm

(photographed in Natural 986)

NEEDLES

1 pair 3¹/4mm (no 10) (US 3) needles
1 pair 3³/4mm (no 9) (US 5) needles
3¹/4mm (no 10) (US 3) circular needle

TENSION

22 sts and 30 rows to 10 cm measured over st st using 3³/4mm (US 5) needles.

FRONT

Using 3¹/4mm (US 3) needles cast on 99 [111: 123: 137] sts.

Row 1 (RS): K1, *P1, K1, rep from * to end.

Row 2: P1, *K1, P1, rep from * to end.

These 2 rows form rib.

Cont in rib for a further 18 rows, ending with RS facing for next row.

Change to 3³/4mm (US 5) needles.

Row 1 (RS): K4 [10: 6: 3], *yfwd, sl 1, K1, psso, K8, rep from * to last 5 [11: 7: 4] sts, yfwd, sl 1, K1, psso, K3 [9: 5: 2].

Row 2: Purl.

These 2 rows form patt.

Cont in patt until front meas 19 [20: 21: 22] cm, ending with RS facing for next row.**

Beg and ending rows as indicated, working chart rows 1 to 52 once only, and then repeating chart rows 53 to 64 throughout as required, now work in patt from chart for front as folls:

Work 32 rows, ending after chart row 32 and with RS facing for next row. (Front should meas 30 [31: 32: 33] cm.)

Divide for neck

Next row (RS): Patt 49 [55: 61: 68] sts and turn, leaving rem sts on a holder.

Work each side of neck separately.

Keeping patt correct, dec 1 st at neck edge on 4th and 12 foll 4th rows. 36 [42: 48: 55] sts.

Work 1 row, ending with RS facing for next row.

(Front should meas 48 [49: 50: 51] cm.)

Shape armhole

Keeping patt correct, cast off 2 [3: 4: 5] sts at beg of next row. 34 [39: 44: 50] sts.

Work 1 row.

Dec 1 st at armhole edge of next 1 [3: 5: 7] rows, then on foll 1 [2: 2: 3] alt rows **and at same time** dec 1 st at neck edge of next and every foll 0 [4th: 4th: 4th] row. 31 [32: 34: 36] sts.

Dec 1 st at front slope edge **only** on 2nd [2nd: 4th: 4th] and 5 [2: 3: 0] foll 4th rows, then on every foll 6th row until 22 [24: 26: 29] sts rem.

Cont straight until armhole meas 18 [19: 20: 21] cm, ending with RS facing for next row.

Shape shoulder

Cast off 7 [8: 9: 10] sts at beg of next and foll alt row.

Work 1 row.

Cast off rem 8 [8: 8: 9] sts.

With RS facing, slip centre st onto a holder, rejoin yarn to rem sts, patt to end.

Complete to match first side, reversing shapings.

BACK

Work as given for front to **.

Beg and ending rows as indicated, working chart rows 1 to 52 once only, and then repeating chart rows 53 to 64 throughout as required, now work in patt from chart for back as folls:

Cont straight until back matches front to beg of armhole shaping, ending with RS facing for next row.

Shape armholes

Keeping patt correct, cast off 2 [3: 4: 5] sts at beg of next 2 rows. 95 [105: 115: 127] sts.

Dec 1 st at each end of next 1 [3: 5: 7] rows, then on foll 1 [2: 2: 3] alt rows. 91 [95: 101: 107] sts.

Cont straight until back matches front to beg of shoulder shaping, ending with RS facing for next row.

Shape shoulders and back neck

Cast off 7 [8: 9: 10] sts at beg of next 2 rows. 77 [79: 83: 87] sts.

Next row (RS): Cast off 7 [8: 9: 10] sts, patt until there are 11 [11: 11: 12] sts on right needle and turn, leaving rem sts on a holder.

Work each side of neck separately.

Cast off 3 sts at beg of next row.

Cast off rem 8 [8: 8: 9] sts.

With RS facing, rejoin yarn to rem sts, cast off centre 41 [41: 43: 43] sts, patt to end.

Complete to match first side, reversing shapings.

SLEEVES

Using 3¹/4mm (US 3) needles cast on 45 [47: 49: 49] sts.

Work in rib as given for back for 6 cm, ending with RS facing for next row.

Change to 3³/4mm (US 5) needles.

Row 1 (RS): K2 [3: 4: 4], *yfwd, sl 1, K1, psso, K8, rep from * to last 3 [4: 5: 5] sts, yfwd, sl 1, K1, psso, K1 [2: 3: 3].

Row 2: Purl.

These 2 rows form patt.

Back

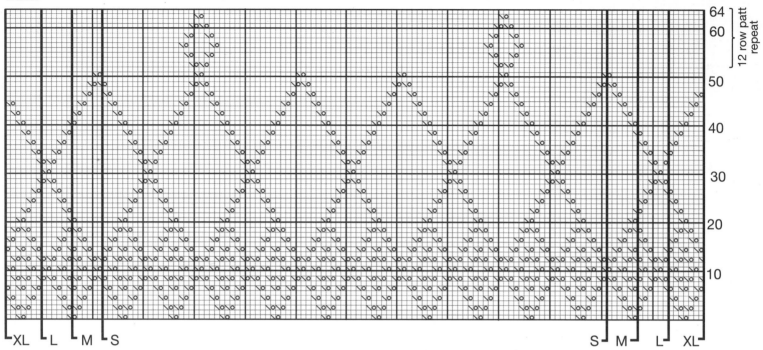

64
60
50
40
30
20
10

12 row patt repeat

XL　L　M　S

S　M　L　XL

Front

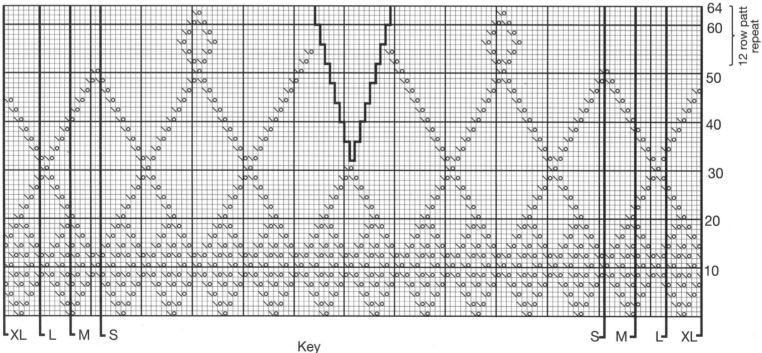

64
60
50
40
30
20
10

12 row patt repeat

XL　L　M　S

S　M　L　XL

Key
☐ K on RS, P on WS
◉ Yfwd
◩ Sl 1, K1, psso

60

Cont in patt, shaping sides by inc 1 st at each end of next and every foll 4th row to 59 [65: 69: 81] sts, then on every foll 6th row until there are 83 [87: 91: 95] sts, taking inc sts into patt.

Cont straight until sleeve meas 44 [45: 46: 46] cm, ending with RS facing for next row.

Shape top

Keeping patt correct, cast off 2 [3: 4: 5] sts at beg of next 2 rows. 79 [81: 83: 85] sts.

Dec 1 st at each end of next 5 rows, then on every foll alt row to 65 sts, then on foll 11 rows, ending with RS facing for next row. 43 sts.

Cast off 5 sts at beg of next 4 rows.

Cast off rem 23 sts.

MAKING UP

Press as described on the information page.

Join right shoulder seam using back stitch, or mattress stitch if preferred.

Neckband

With RS facing and using 3¼mm (US 3) circular needle, pick up and knit 96 [98: 100: 104] sts down left side of neck, K st from holder at base of V and mark this st with a coloured thread, pick up and knit 96 [98: 100: 104] sts up right side of neck, then 47 [47: 49: 49] sts from back. 240 [244: 250: 258] sts.

Round 1 (RS): *K1, P1, rep from * to end.

This round sets position of rib.

Keeping rib correct, cont as folls:

Round 2: Rib to within 1 st of marked st, slip 2 sts as though to K2tog (marked st is 2nd of these 2 sts), K1, pass 2 slipped sts over, rib to end.

Rep last round 3 times more.

Cast off in rib, still decreasing either side of marked st as before.

See information page for finishing instructions, setting in sleeves using the set-in method.

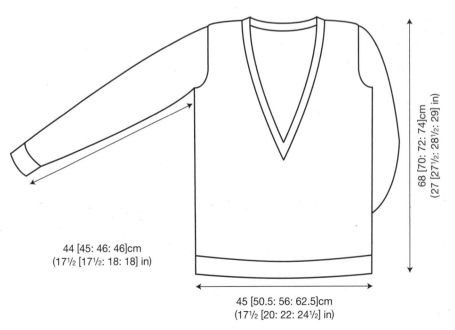

44 [45: 46: 46]cm
(17½ [17½: 18: 18] in)

68 [70: 72: 74]cm
(27 [27½: 28½: 29] in)

45 [50.5: 56: 62.5]cm
(17½ [20: 22: 24½] in)

sweet william

main image page 23

SIZE

8	10	12	14	16	18	20	22	
To fit bust								
81	86	91	97	102	107	112	117	in
32	34	36	38	40	42	44	46	cm

YARN

Rowan Purelife Organic Cotton

10	11	11	12	12	13	14	14	x 50gm

(photographed in Lipstick Tree 985)

NEEDLES

1 pair 3¼mm (no 10) (US 3) needles
1 pair 3¾mm (no 9) (US 5) needles
Cable needle

TENSION

28 sts and 34 rows to 10 cm measured over body patt using 3¾mm (US 5) needles. 23 sts and 48 rows to 10 cm measured over sleeve patt using 3¾mm (US 5) needles.

Pattern note: When working **body patt**, all slipped sts should be slipped with yarn at WS (back on RS rows, front on WS rows) of work.

BACK

Using 3¼mm (US 3) needles cast on 92 [98: 104: 110: 116: 122: 128: 134] sts.

Row 1 (RS): K2, *P1, K2, rep from * to end.

Row 2: P2, *K1, P2, rep from * to end.

These 2 rows form rib.

Work in rib for a further 4 rows, ending with RS facing for next row.

Change to 3¾mm (US 5) needles.

Row 7 (RS): K0 [3: 10: 6: 5: 5: 4: 4], (K2, M1, K3, M1, K2) 13 [13: 12: 14: 15: 16: 17: 18] times, K1 [4: 10: 6: 6: 5: 5: 4].

118 [124: 128: 138: 146: 154: 162: 170] sts.

Now work in body patt as folls:

Row 1 (WS): P2 [2: 1: 3: 1: 2: 3: 1], *P next st winding yarn twice round needle, P4, P next st winding yarn twice round needle, rep from * to last 2 [2: 1: 3: 1: 2: 3: 1] sts, P2 [2: 1: 3: 1: 2: 3: 1].

Row 2: K2 [2: 1: 3: 1: 2: 3: 1], *sl 1 dropping extra loop, K4, sl 1 dropping extra loop, rep from * to last 2 [2: 1: 3: 1: 2: 3: 1] sts, K2 [2: 1: 3: 1: 2: 3: 1].

Row 3: P2 [2: 1: 3: 1: 2: 3: 1], *sl 1, P4, sl 1, rep from * to last 2 [2: 1: 3: 1: 2: 3: 1] sts, P2 [2: 1: 3: 1: 2: 3: 1].

Row 4: K2 [2: 1: 3: 1: 2: 3: 1], *sl 1, K4, sl 1, rep from * to last 2 [2: 1: 3: 1: 2: 3: 1] sts, K2 [2: 1: 3: 1: 2: 3: 1].

Row 5: As row 3.

Row 6: K2 [2: 1: 3: 1: 2: 3: 1], *slip next st onto cable needle and leave at front of work, K2, then K1 from cable needle, slip next 2 sts onto cable needle and leave at back of work, K1, then K2 from cable needle,

rep from * to last 2 [2: 1: 3: 1: 2: 3: 1] sts, K2 [2: 1: 3: 1: 2: 3: 1].

These 6 rows form body patt.

Cont in body patt until back meas 34 [34: 33: 36: 35: 37: 36: 38] cm, ending with RS facing for next row.

Shape armholes

Keeping patt correct, cast off 4 [5: 5: 6: 6: 7: 7: 8] sts at beg of next 2 rows.

110 [114: 118: 126: 134: 140: 148: 154] sts.

Dec 1 st at each end of next 5 [5: 7: 7: 9: 9: 11: 11] rows, then on foll 4 [4: 3: 5: 5: 6: 6: 6] alt rows.

92 [96: 98: 102: 106: 110: 114: 120] sts.

Cont straight until armhole meas 18 [18: 19: 19: 20: 20: 21: 21] cm, ending with RS facing for next row.

Shape shoulders and back neck

Cast off 6 [7: 7: 8: 8: 9: 10: 11] sts at beg of next 2 rows. 80 [82: 84: 86: 90: 92: 94: 98] sts.

Next row (RS): Cast off 6 [7: 7: 8: 8: 9: 10: 11] sts, patt until there are 11 [11: 12: 12: 13: 13: 13: 14] sts on right needle and turn, leaving rem sts on a holder.

Work each side of neck separately.

Cast off 4 sts at beg of next row.

Cast off rem 7 [7: 8: 8: 9: 9: 9: 10] sts.

With RS facing, rejoin yarn to rem sts, cast off centre 46 [46: 46: 46: 48: 48: 48: 48] sts, patt to end.

Complete to match first side, reversing shapings.

FRONT

Work as given for back until 32 [32: 32: 34: 34: 34: 36: 36] rows less have been worked than on back to beg of shoulder shaping, ending with RS facing for next row.

Shape neck

Next row (RS): Patt 33 [35: 36: 39: 40: 42: 45: 48] sts and turn, leaving rem sts on a holder.

Work each side of neck separately.

Keeping patt correct, dec 1 st at neck edge of next 6 rows, then on foll 6 [6: 6: 7: 7: 7: 8: 8] alt rows, then on 2 foll 4th rows. 19 [21: 22: 24: 25: 27: 29: 32] sts.

Work 5 rows, ending with RS facing for next row.

Shape shoulder

Cast off 6 [7: 7: 8: 8: 9: 10: 11] sts at beg of next and foll alt row.

Work 1 row.

Cast off rem 7 [7: 8: 8: 9: 9: 9: 10] sts.

With RS facing, rejoin yarn to rem sts, cast off centre 26 [26: 26: 24: 26: 26: 24: 24] sts, patt to end.

Complete to match first side, reversing shapings.

Pattern note: When working **sleeve patt**, all slipped sts should be slipped with yarn at RS (front) of work. Do **NOT** pull yarn tight across RS of work but leave strand 'floating' across front of work.

SLEEVES

Using 3¼mm (US 3) needles cast on 50 [50: 53: 53: 53: 53: 56: 56] sts.

Work in rib as given for back for 6 rows, inc 2 [2: 1: 1: 3: 3: 2: 2] sts evenly across last row and ending with RS facing for next row.

52 [52: 54: 54: 56: 56: 58: 58] sts.

Change to 3¾mm (US 5) needles.

Row 7 (RS): Knit.

Now work in sleeve patt as folls:

Row 1 and every foll alt row: Purl.

Row 2 (RS): K1 [1: 1: 1: 2: 2: 3: 3], (sl 1) 1 [1: 2: 2: 2: 2: 2: 2] times, *(sl 1) twice, K2, (sl 1) twice, rep from * to last 2 [2: 3: 3: 4: 4: 5: 5] sts, (sl 1) 1 [1: 2: 2: 2: 2: 2: 2] times, K1 [1: 1: 1: 2: 2: 3: 3].

Row 4: As row 2.

Row 6: Inc in first st, K0 [0: 0: 0: 1: 1: 2: 2], (sl 1) 1 [1: 2: 2: 2: 2: 2: 2] times, *(sl 1) twice, K2, (sl 1) twice, rep from * to last 2 [2: 3: 3: 4: 4: 5: 5] sts, (sl 1) 1 [1: 2: 2: 2: 2: 2: 2] times, K0 [0: 0: 0: 1: 1: 2: 2], inc in last st. 54 [54: 56: 56: 58: 58: 60: 60] sts.

Row 8: K1 [1: 2: 2: 3: 3: 4: 4], (sl 1) twice, *(sl 1) twice, K2, (sl 1) twice, rep from * to last 3 [3: 4: 4: 5: 5: 6: 6] sts, (sl 1) twice, K1 [1: 2: 2: 3: 3: 4: 4].

Row 10: K1, (sl 1) 1 [1: 2: 2: 3: 3: 4: 4] times, K1, *K1, (sl 1) 4 times, K1, rep from * to last 3 [3: 4: 4: 5: 5: 6: 6] sts, K1, (sl 1) 1 [1: 2: 2: 3: 3: 4: 4] times, K1.

Row 12: AS row 10.

Row 14: Inc in first st, (sl 1) 1 [1: 2: 2: 3: 3: 4: 4] times, K1, *K1, (sl 1) 4 times, K1, rep from * to last 3 [3: 4: 4: 5: 5: 6: 6] sts, K1, (sl 1) 1 [1: 2: 2: 3: 3: 4: 4] times, inc in last st. 56 [56: 58: 58: 60: 60: 62: 62] sts.

Row 16: K1 [1: 1: 1: 1: 1: 2: 2], (sl 1) 2 [2: 3: 3: 4: 4: 4: 4] times, K1, *K1, (sl 1) 4 times, K1, rep from * to last 4 [4: 5: 5: 6: 6: 7: 7] sts, K1, (sl 1) 2 [2: 3: 3: 4: 4: 4: 4] times, K1 [1: 1: 1: 1: 1: 2: 2].

These 16 rows form sleeve patt.

Cont in patt, shaping sides by inc 1 st at each end of 8th [6th: 6th: 6th: 6th: 6th: 6th: 6th] and every foll 10th [8th: 8th: 8th: 8th: 8th: 8th: 8th] row to 88 [66: 64: 74: 72: 82: 88: 98] sts, then on every foll – [10th: 10th: 10th: 10th: 10th: 10th: 10th] row until there are – [90: 92: 94: 96: 98: 100: 102] sts, taking inc sts into patt.

Cont straight until sleeve meas 44 [44: 45: 45: 46: 46: 45: 45] cm, ending with RS facing for next row.

Shape top

Keeping patt correct, cast off 3 [4: 4: 5: 5: 6: 6: 7] sts at beg of next 2 rows.

82 [82: 84: 84: 86: 86: 88: 88] sts.

Dec 1 st at each end of next 3 rows, then on every foll alt row to 36 sts, then on foll 9 rows, ending with RS facing for next row.

Cast off rem 18 sts.

MAKING UP

Press as described on the information page.

Join right shoulder seam using back stitch, or mattress stitch if preferred.

Neckband

With RS facing and using 3¼mm (US 3) needles, pick up and knit 29 [29: 29: 31: 31: 31: 33: 33] sts down left side of neck, 21 [21: 21: 20: 21: 21: 20: 20] sts from front, 29 [29: 29: 31: 31: 31: 33: 33] sts up right side of neck, then 43 [43: 43: 43: 45: 45: 45: 45] sts from back.

122 [122: 122: 125: 128: 128: 131: 131] sts.

Beg with row 2, work in rib as given for back for 5 rows, ending with RS facing for next row.

Cast off in rib.

See information page for finishing instructions, setting in sleeves using the set-in method.

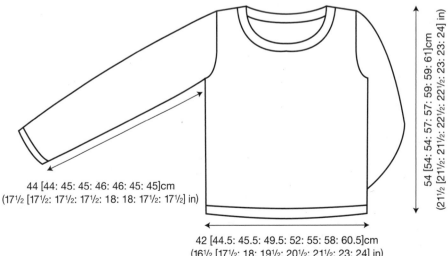

44 [44: 45: 45: 46: 46: 45: 45]cm
(17½ [17½: 17½: 17½: 18: 18: 17½: 17½] in)

42 [44.5: 45.5: 49.5: 52: 55: 58: 60.5]cm
(16½ [17½: 18: 19½: 20½: 21½: 23: 24] in)

54 [54: 54: 57: 57: 59: 59: 61]cm
(21½ [21½: 21½: 22½: 22½: 23: 23: 24] in)

cedar

main image page 26

SIZE

S	M	L	XL	XXL	
To fit chest					
102	107	112	117	122	cm
40	42	44	46	48	in

YARN

Rowan Purelife Organic Cotton

18	19	20	21	22	x 50gm

(photographed in Logwood 981)

NEEDLES

1 pair 3¼mm (no 10) (US 3) needles
1 pair 3¾mm (no 9) (US 5) needles
Cable needle

TENSION

30 sts and 32 rows to 10 cm measured over patt using 3¾mm (US 5) needles.

SPECIAL ABBREVIATIONS

C3B = slip next st onto cable needle and leave at back of work, K2, then K1 from cable needle; **C3F** = slip next 2 sts onto cable needle and leave at front of work, K1, then K2 from cable needle; **Cr3R** = slip next st onto cable needle and leave at back of work, K2, then P1 from cable needle; **Cr3L** = slip next 2 sts onto cable needle and leave at front of work, P1, then K2 from cable needle; **Cr4R** = slip next 2 sts onto cable needle and leave at back of work, K2, then P2 from cable needle; **Cr4L** = slip next 2 sts onto cable needle and leave at front of work, P2, then K2 from cable needle; **C4B** = slip next 2 sts onto cable needle and leave at back of work, K2, then K2 from cable needle; **C4F** = slip next 2 sts onto cable needle and leave at front of work, K2, then K2 from cable needle.

BACK

Using 3¼mm (US 3) needles cast on 126 [134: 138: 146: 154] sts.

Row 1 (RS): K2, *P2, K2, rep from * to end.
Row 2: P2, *K2, P2, rep from * to end.
These 2 rows form rib.

Work in rib for a further 17 rows, ending with **WS** facing for next row.

Row 20 (WS): Rib 4 [8: 1: 5: 6], M1, (rib 3, M1) 39 [39: 45: 45: 47] times, rib to end.
166 [174: 184: 192: 202] sts.

Change to 3¾mm (US 5) needles.

Beg and ending rows as indicated and repeating the 28 row patt rep throughout, now work in patt from chart for body as folls:

Cont straight until back meas 41 [42: 41: 42: 41] cm, ending with RS facing for next row.

Shape armholes

Keeping patt correct, cast off 3 sts at beg of next 2 rows. 160 [168: 178: 186: 196] sts.

Dec 1 st at each end of next 5 [3: 3: 1: 1] rows, then on foll 3 [3: 2: 2: 1] alt rows.
144 [156: 168: 180: 192] sts.

Cont straight until armhole meas 23 [24: 25: 26: 27] cm, ending with RS facing for next row.

Shape shoulders and back neck

Cast off 14 [16: 18: 20: 22] sts at beg of next 2 rows. 116 [124: 132: 140: 148] sts.

Next row (RS): Cast off 14 [16: 18: 20: 22] sts, patt until there are 19 [21: 22: 24: 25] sts on right needle and turn, leaving rem sts on a holder.

Work each side of neck separately.

Cast off 4 sts at beg of next row.

Cast off rem 15 [17: 18: 20: 21] sts.

With RS facing, rejoin yarn to rem sts, cast off centre 50 [50: 52: 52: 54] sts, patt to end.

Complete to match first side, reversing shapings.

FRONT

Work as given for back until 16 [16: 18: 18: 20] rows less have been worked than on back to beg of shoulder shaping, ending with RS facing for next row.

Shape neck

Next row (RS): Patt 53 [59: 65: 71: 77] sts and turn, leaving rem sts on a holder.

Work each side of neck separately.

Keeping patt correct, dec 1 st at neck edge of next 8 rows, then on foll 2 [2: 3: 3: 4] alt rows.
43 [49: 54: 60: 65] sts.

Work 3 rows, ending with RS facing for next row.

Shape shoulder

Cast off 14 [16: 18: 20: 22] sts at beg of next and foll alt row.

Work 1 row.

Cast off rem 15 [17: 18: 20: 21] sts.

With RS facing, rejoin yarn to rem sts, cast off centre 38 sts, patt to end.

Complete to match first side, reversing shapings.

SLEEVES

Using 3¼mm (US 3) needles cast on 50 [50: 54: 54: 58] sts.

Work in rib as given for back for 19 rows, ending with WS facing for next row.

Row 20 (WS): Rib 5 [2: 4: 1: 3], M1, (rib 3, M1) 13 [15: 15: 17: 17] times, rib to end.
64 [66: 70: 72: 76] sts.

Change to 3¾mm (US 5) needles.

Beg and ending rows as indicated and repeating the 16 row patt rep throughout, now work in patt from chart for sleeve as folls:

Inc 1 st at each end of 3rd and foll 16 [13: 7: 4: 0] alt rows, then on every foll 4th row until there are 148 [150: 152: 154: 156] sts, taking inc sts into patt.

Cont straight until sleeve meas 53 [55: 57: 59: 61] cm, ending with RS facing for next row.

Shape top

Keeping patt correct, cast off 3 sts at beg of next 28 rows.

Cast off rem 64 [66: 68: 70: 72] sts.

MAKING UP

Press as described on the information page.

Join right shoulder seam using back stitch, or mattress stitch if preferred.

Neckband

With RS facing and using 3¼mm (US 3) needles, pick up and knit 16 [16: 17: 17: 20] sts down left side of neck, 28 sts from front, 16 [16: 17: 17: 20] sts up right side of neck, then 50 [50: 52: 52: 54] sts from back.
110 [110: 114: 114: 122] sts.

Beg with row 2, work in rib as given for back for 7 rows, ending with RS facing for next row.

Cast off in rib.

See information page for finishing instructions, setting in sleeves using the shallow set-in method.

Body Chart

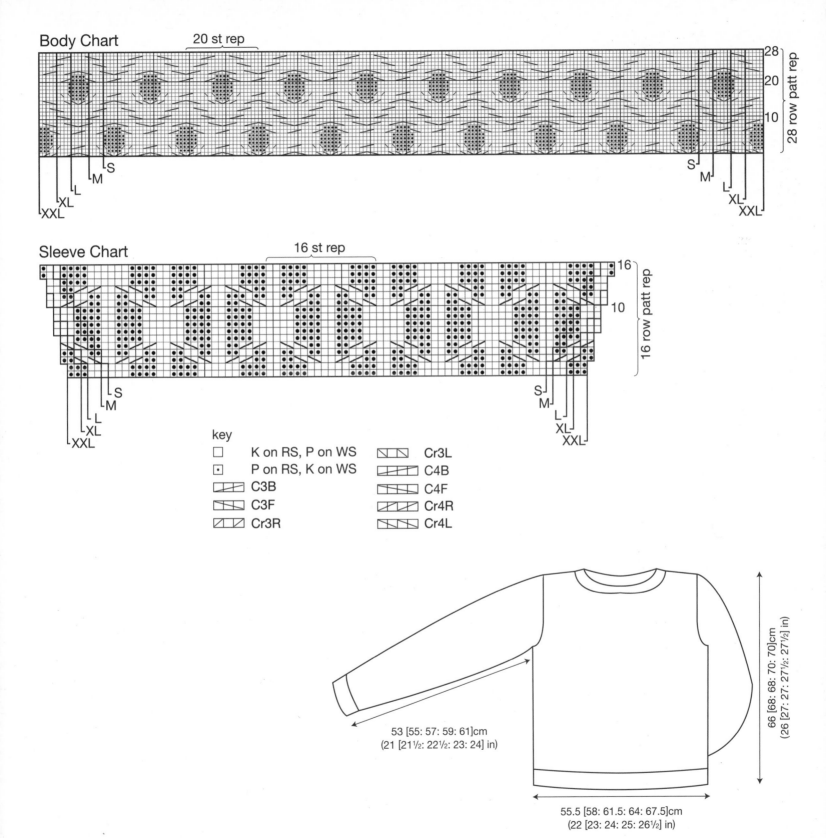

20 st rep

28
20
10

28 row patt rep

S
M
L
XL
XXL

Sleeve Chart

16 st rep

16
10

16 row patt rep

S
M
L
XL
XXL

key

☐	K on RS, P on WS	
⊡	P on RS, K on WS	
	C3B	Cr3L
	C3F	C4B
	Cr3R	C4F
		Cr4R
		Cr4L

53 [55: 57: 59: 61]cm
(21 [21½: 22½: 23: 24] in)

66 [68: 68: 70: 70]cm
(26 [27: 27: 27½: 27½] in)

55.5 [58: 61.5: 64: 67.5]cm
(22 [23: 24: 25: 26½] in)

busy lizzie

main image page 29

SIZE

	S	M	L	XL	
To fit bust					
	81-86	91-97	102-107	112-117	cm
	32-34	36-38	40-42	44-46	in

YARN

Rowan Purelife Organic Cotton

	9	10	10	11	x 50gm

(photographed in Quebracho Bark 987)

NEEDLES

1 pair 3¹/4mm (no 10) (US 3) needles
1 pair 3³/4mm (no 9) (US 5) needles

BUTTONS

2 x 00421

TENSION

22 sts and 30 rows to 10 cm measured over st st
using 3³/4mm (US 5) needles.

BACK

Using 3¹/4mm (US 3) needles cast on 107 [119: 133: 145] sts.

Row 1 (RS): K1, *P1, K1, rep from * to end.

Row 2: As row 1.

These 2 rows form moss st.

Work in moss st for 7 cm, ending with RS facing for next row.

Change to 3³/4mm (US 5) needles.

Beg with a K row, work in st st until back meas 21 [22: 23: 24] cm, ending with RS facing for next row.

Shape for cap sleeves

Inc 1 st at each end of next and foll alt row, then on 7 foll rows, ending with **WS** facing for next row.
125 [137: 151: 163] sts.

Cont straight until armhole meas 21 [22: 23: 24] cm **from last inc**, ending with RS facing for next row.

Shape shoulders and back neck

Cast off 7 [8: 9: 10] sts at beg of next 4 rows.
97 [105: 115: 123] sts.

Next row (RS): Cast off 7 [8: 9: 10] sts, K until there are 26 [29: 32: 35] sts on right needle and turn, leaving rem sts on a holder.

Work each side of neck separately.

Dec 1 st at neck edge of next 5 rows, ending with RS facing for next row, **and at same time** cast off 7 [8: 9: 10] sts at beg of 2nd and foll alt row.

Cast off rem 7 [8: 9: 10] sts.

With RS facing, rejoin yarn to rem sts, cast off centre 31 [31: 33: 33] sts, K to end.

Complete to match first side, reversing shapings.

LEFT FRONT

Using 3¹/4mm (US 3) needles cast on 82 [88: 95: 101] sts.

Row 1 (RS): *K1, P1, rep from * to last 0 [0: 1: 1] st, K0 [0: 1: 1].

Row 2: K0 [0: 1: 1], *P1, K1, rep from * to end.

These 2 rows form moss st.

Work in moss st for 7 cm, ending with RS facing for next row.

Change to 3³/4mm (US 5) needles.

Next row (RS): K to last 9 sts, moss st 9 sts.

Next row: Moss st 9 sts, P to end.

These 2 rows set the sts.

Cont as set until left front meas 21 [22: 23: 24] cm, ending with RS facing for next row.

Shape for cap sleeve

Keeping sts correct, inc 1 st at beg of next and foll alt row, then at same edge on 7 foll rows, ending with **WS** facing for next row. 91 [97: 104: 110] sts.

Cont straight until armhole meas 21 [22: 23: 24] cm **from last inc**, ending with RS facing for next row.

Shape shoulder and neck

Cast off 7 [8: 9: 10] sts at beg of next and foll alt row.
77 [81: 86: 90] sts.

Work 1 row, ending with RS facing for next row.

Next row (RS): Cast off 7 [8: 9: 10] sts, K until there are 26 [29: 32: 35] sts on right needle and turn, leaving rem 44 [44: 45: 45] sts on a holder.

Dec 1 st at neck edge of next 5 rows, ending with RS facing for next row, **and at same time** cast off 7 [8: 9: 10] sts at beg of 2nd and foll alt row.

Cast off rem 7 [8: 9: 10] sts.

RIGHT FRONT

Using 3¹/4mm (US 3) needles cast on 82 [88: 95: 101] sts.

Row 1 (RS): K0 [0: 1: 1], *P1, K1, rep from * to end.

Row 2: *K1, P1, rep from * to last 0 [0: 1: 1] st, K0 [0: 1: 1].

These 2 rows form moss st.

Work in moss st for 7 cm, ending with RS facing for next row.

Change to 3³/4mm (US 5) needles.

Next row (RS): Moss st 9 sts, K to end.

Next row: P to last 9 sts, moss st 9 sts.

These 2 rows set the sts.

Cont as set until right front meas 21 [22: 23: 24] cm, ending with RS facing for next row.

Shape for cap sleeve

Keeping sts correct, inc 1 st at end of next and foll alt row, then at same edge on 7 foll rows, ending with **WS** facing for next row. 91 [97: 104: 110] sts.

Work 9 rows, ending with RS facing for next row.

Next row (RS): Moss st 9 sts, cast off 4 sts (for first buttonhole), K until there are 34 sts on right needle after cast-off, cast off 4 sts (for 2nd buttonhole), K to end.

Next row: Patt to end, casting on 4 sts over those cast off on previous row.

Cont straight until armhole meas 21 [22: 23: 24] cm **from last inc**, ending with **WS** facing for next row.

Shape shoulder and neck

Cast off 7 [8: 9: 10] sts at beg of next and foll alt row, ending with RS facing for next row.
77 [81: 86: 90] sts.

Next row (RS): Patt 44 [44: 45: 45] sts and slip these sts onto a holder, K to end. 33 [37: 41: 45] sts.
Dec 1 st at neck edge of next 5 rows, ending with RS facing for next row, **and at same time** cast off 7 [8: 9: 10] sts at beg of next and foll 2 alt rows.
Work 1 row.
Cast off rem 7 [8: 9: 10] sts.

MAKING UP

Press as described on the information page.
Join both shoulder seams using back stitch, or mattress stitch if preferred.

Neckband

With RS facing and using 3¼mm (US 3) needles, slip 44 [44: 45: 45] sts from right front holder onto right needle, rejoin yarn and pick up and knit 5 sts up right side of neck, 41 [41: 43: 43] sts from back, and 5 sts down left side of neck, then patt across 44 [44: 45: 45] sts from left front holder. 139 [139: 143: 143] sts.
Row 1 (WS): Knit.
Cast off knitwise.
Armhole borders (both alike)
With RS facing and using 3¼mm (US 3) needles, beg and ending level with last cap sleeve inc, pick up and knit 91 [95: 101: 105] sts evenly along entire armhole edge.
Work in moss st as given for back, dec 1 st at each end of next 3 rows, then on foll 3 alt rows, then on 3 foll 4th rows. 73 [77: 83: 87] sts.
Cont straight until border meas 7 cm from pick-up row, ending with RS facing for next row.
Cast off in moss st.
See information page for finishing instructions, attaching buttons to left front so that, when fastened, fronts overlap by 26 cm.

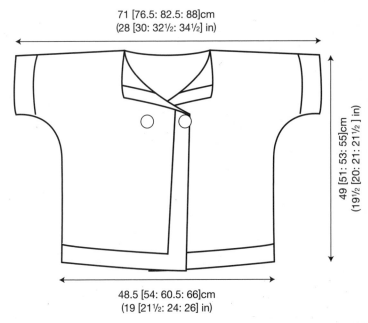

71 [76.5: 82.5: 88]cm
(28 [30: 32½: 34½] in)

49 [51: 53: 55]cm
(19½ [20: 21: 21½] in)

48.5 [54: 60.5: 66]cm
(19 [21½: 24: 26] in)

snapdragon

main image page 31

SIZE

8	10	12	14	16	18	20	22	
To fit bust								
81	86	91	97	102	107	112	117	in
32	34	36	38	40	42	44	46	cm

YARN

Rowan Purelife Organic Cotton

8	8	9	9	10	10	11	11	x 50gm

(photographed in Quebracho Bark 987)

NEEDLES

1 pair 3¼mm (no 10) (US 3) needles
1 pair 3¾mm (no 9) (US 5) needles

TENSION

22 sts and 30 rows to 10 cm measured over st st
using 3¾mm (US 5) needles.

BACK

Using 3¼mm (US 3) needles cast on 93 [97: 101: 107: 115: 121: 127: 135] sts.

Row 1 (RS): K1, *P1, K1, rep from * to end.

Row 2: As row 1.

These 2 rows form moss st.

Cont in moss st for a further 4 rows, ending with RS facing for next row.

Change to 3¾mm (US 5) needles.

Row 7 (RS): (K1, P1) twice, K to last 4 sts, (P1, K1) twice.

Row 8: (K1, P1) twice, P to last 4 sts, (P1, K1) twice.

Rep last 2 rows 5 times more, ending with RS facing for next row.

Beg with a K row, work in st st until back meas 28 [28: 27: 30: 29: 31: 30: 32] cm, ending with RS facing for next row.

Beg and ending rows as indicated and repeating the 36 row patt rep throughout, work from chart as folls:

Work straight until back meas 34 [34: 33: 36: 35: 37: 36: 38] cm, ending with RS facing for next row.

Shape armholes

Keeping chart correct, cast off 3 [4: 4: 5: 5: 6: 6: 7] sts at beg of next 2 rows. 87 [89: 93: 97: 105: 109: 115: 121] sts. (**Note:** Armhole shaping is **NOT** shown on chart.)

Dec 1 st at each end of next 3 [3: 5: 5: 7: 7: 9: 9] rows, then on foll 4 [4: 3: 3: 4: 4: 3: 5] alt rows. 73 [75: 77: 81: 83: 87: 91: 93] sts.

Cont straight until armhole meas 18 [18: 19: 19: 20: 20: 21: 21] cm, ending with RS facing for next row.

Shape shoulders and back neck

Cast off 5 [5: 6: 6: 6: 7: 8: 8] sts at beg of next 2 rows. 63 [65: 65: 69: 71: 73: 75: 77] sts.

Next row (RS): Cast off 5 [5: 6: 6: 6: 7: 8: 8] sts, patt until there are 8 [9: 8: 10: 10: 10: 10: 11] sts on right needle and turn, leaving rem sts on a holder.

Work each side of neck separately.

Cast off 3 sts at beg of next row.

Cast off rem 5 [6: 5: 7: 7: 7: 7: 8] sts.

With RS facing, rejoin yarn to rem sts, cast off centre 37 [37: 37: 37: 39: 39: 39: 39] sts, patt to end.

Complete to match first side, reversing shapings.

FRONT

Work as given for back until 28 [28: 28: 30: 30: 30: 32: 32] rows less have been worked than on back to beg of shoulder shaping, ending with RS facing for next row.

Shape neck

Next row (RS): Patt 28 [29: 30: 33: 33: 35: 38: 39] sts and turn, leaving rem sts on a holder.

Work each side of neck separately.

Keeping patt correct, dec 1 st at neck edge of next 8 rows, then on foll 3 [3: 3: 4: 4: 4: 5: 5] alt rows, then on 2 foll 4th rows. 15 [16: 17: 19: 19: 21: 23: 24] sts.

Work 5 rows, ending with RS facing for next row.

Shape shoulder

Cast off 5 [5: 6: 6: 6: 7: 8: 8] sts at beg of next and foll alt row.

Work 1 row.

Cast off rem 5 [6: 5: 7: 7: 7: 7: 8] sts.

With RS facing, rejoin yarn to rem sts, cast off centre 17 [17: 17: 15: 17: 17: 15: 15] sts, patt to end.

Complete to match first side, reversing shapings.

SLEEVES

Using 3¼mm (US 3) needles cast on 49 [49: 51: 51: 53: 53: 55: 55] sts.

Work in moss st as given for back for 6 rows, ending with RS facing for next row.

Change to 3¾mm (US 5) needles.

Beg and ending rows as indicated, work from chart, shaping sides by inc 1 st at each end of 5th [3rd: 5th: 3rd: 3rd: 3rd: 3rd: 3rd] and every foll 6th [6th: 6th: 4th: 6th: 4th: 4th: 4th] row to 61 [61: 63: 57: 65: 61: 67: 73] sts, then on every foll – [-: -: 6th: -: 6th: 6th: -] row until there are – [-: -: 65: -: 67: 71: -] sts, taking inc sts into patt.

Work 1 [3: 1: 1: 3: 3: 1: 1] rows, ending after chart row 36 and with RS facing for next row.

Beg with a K row, work in st st, shaping sides by inc 1 st at each end of 5th [3rd: 5th: 5th: 3rd: 3rd: 5th: 5th] and every foll 6th row to 81 [87: 89: 91: 93: 95: 97: 99] sts, then on every foll 8th [-: -: -: -: -: -: -] row until there are 85 [-: -: -: -: -: -: -] sts.

Cont straight until sleeve meas 44 [44: 45: 45: 46: 46: 45: 45] cm, ending with RS facing for next row.

Shape top

Cast off 3 [4: 4: 5: 5: 6: 6: 7] sts at beg of next 2 rows. 79 [79: 81: 81: 83: 83: 85: 85] sts.

Dec 1 st at each end of next 5 rows, then on every foll alt row to 57 sts, then on foll 11 rows, ending with RS facing for next row. 35 sts.

Cast off 6 sts at beg of next 2 rows.

Cast off rem 23 sts.

MAKING UP

Press as described on the information page.

Join right shoulder seam using back stitch, or mattress stitch if preferred.

Neckband

With RS facing and using 3¼mm (US 3) needles, pick up and knit 28 [28: 28: 30: 30: 30: 32: 32] sts down left side of neck, 17 [17: 17: 15: 17: 17: 15: 15] sts from front, 28 [28: 28: 30: 30: 30: 32: 32] sts up right side of neck, then 42 [42: 42: 42: 44: 44: 44: 44] sts from back.

115 [115: 115: 117: 121: 121: 123: 123] sts.

Work in moss st as given for back for 5 rows, ending with RS facing for next row.

Cast off in moss st.

See information page for finishing instructions, setting in sleeves using the set-in method and leaving side seams open for first 18 rows.

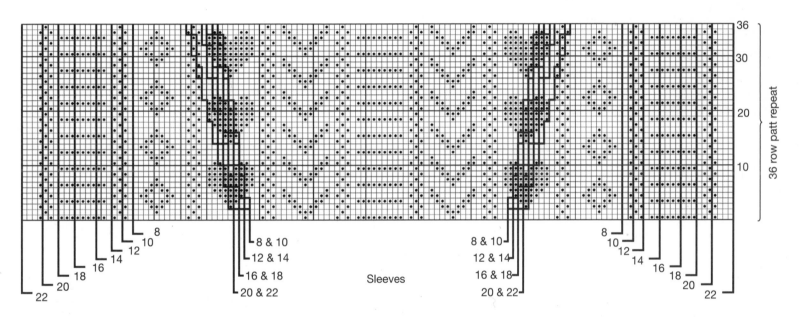

Sleeves

36 row patt repeat

8
10
12
14
16
18
20
22

8 & 10
12 & 14
16 & 18
20 & 22

8 & 10
12 & 14
16 & 18
20 & 22

8
10
12
14
16
18
20
22

Key
☐ K on RS, P on WS
☒ P on RS, K on WS

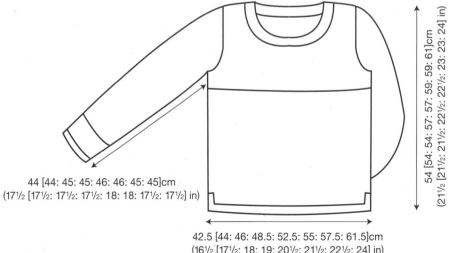

44 [44: 45: 45: 46: 46: 45: 45]cm
(17½ [17½: 17½: 17½: 18: 18: 17½: 17½] in)

42.5 [44: 46: 48.5: 52.5: 55: 57.5: 61.5]cm
(16½ [17½: 18: 19: 20½: 21½: 22½: 24] in)

54 [54: 54: 57: 57: 59: 59: 61]cm
(21½ [21½: 21½: 22½: 22½: 23: 23: 24] in)

sycamore 🌿🌿
main image page 33

SIZE

S	M	L	XL	XXL
To fit chest				
102	107	112	117	122	cm
40	42	44	46	48	in

YARN

Rowan Purelife Organic Cotton

| 14 | 15 | 16 | 17 | 18 | x 50gm |

(photographed in Logwood 981)

NEEDLES

1 pair 3¹/₄mm (no 10) (US 3) needles
1 pair 3³/₄mm (no 9) (US 5) needles
3¹/₄mm (no 10) (US 3) circular needle
Cable needle

TENSION

22 sts and 30 rows to 10 cm measured over st st using 3³/₄mm (US 5) needles.

SPECIAL ABBREVIATIONS

C4B = slip next 2 sts onto cable needle and leave at back of work, K2, then K2 from cable needle;
C4F = slip next 2 sts onto cable needle and leave at front of work, K2, then K2 from cable needle.

BACK

Using 3¹/₄mm (US 3) needles cast on 122 [126: 134: 142: 146] sts.

Row 1 (RS): K2, *P2, K2, rep from * to end.
Row 2: P2, *K2, P2, rep from * to end.
These 2 rows form rib.

Work in rib for a further 18 rows, dec [inc: inc: dec: inc] 1 st at end of last row and ending with RS facing for next row. 121 [127: 135: 141: 147] sts.
Change to 3³/₄mm (US 5) needles.
Beg with a K row, work in st st until back measures 13 cm, ending with **WS** facing for next row.
Next row (WS): P25 [28: 32: 35: 38], M1P, (P5, M1P) twice, P4, M1P, P11, M1P, P21, M1P, P11, M1P, P4, (M1P, P5) twice, M1P, P to end.
131 [137: 145: 151: 157] sts.
Now work in patt as folls:
Row 1 (RS): K16 [19: 23: 26: 29], work next 99 sts as row 1 of chart for body, K to end.
Row 2: P16 [19: 23: 26: 29], work next 99 sts as row 2 of chart for body, P to end.
These 2 rows set the sts – central chart with st st at sides.
Keeping sts correct and repeating the 20 row patt rep throughout, cont as set until back meas 41 [42: 41: 42: 41] cm, ending with RS facing for next row.

Shape armholes

Keeping patt correct, cast off 2 sts at beg of next 2 rows. 127 [133: 141: 147: 153] sts.
Dec 1 st at each end of next 3 [3: 3: 1: 1] rows, then on foll 3 [1: 1: 1: 0] alt rows.
115 [125: 133: 143: 151] sts.
Cont straight until armhole meas 21 [22: 23: 24: 25] cm, ending with RS facing for next row.

Shape back saddle shoulders

Cast off 12 [14: 15: 17: 18] sts at beg of next 4 rows, then 13 [14: 15: 16: 17] sts at beg of foll 2 rows.
Cast off rem 41 [41: 43: 43: 45] sts, placing markers either side of centre 29 [29: 31: 31: 33] sts.

FRONT

Work as given for back until 10 rows less have been worked than on back to beg of saddle shoulder shaping, ending with RS facing for next row.

Shape neck

Next row (RS): Patt 44 [49: 52: 57: 60] sts and turn, leaving rem sts on a holder.
Work each side of neck separately.
Dec 1 st at neck edge of next 3 rows, ending with RS facing for next row. 41 [46: 49: 54: 57] sts.

Shape front saddle shoulder

Dec 1 st at neck edge of next 4 rows **and at same time** cast off 12 [14: 15: 17: 18] sts at beg of next and foll alt row.
Cast off rem 13 [14: 15: 16: 17] sts.
With RS facing, rejoin yarn to rem sts, cast off centre 27 [27: 29: 29: 31] sts, patt to end.
Complete to match first side, reversing shapings.

SLEEVES

Using 3¹/₄mm (US 3) needles cast on 46 [46: 50: 50: 54] sts.
Work in rib as given for back for 20 rows, inc 0 [1: 0: 1: 0] st at each end of last row and ending with RS facing for next row. 46 [48: 50: 52: 54] sts.
Change to 3³/₄mm (US 5) needles.
Beg with a K row, work in st st, inc 1 st at each end of 3rd and 4 foll 4th rows, ending with **WS** facing for next row. 56 [58: 60: 62: 64] sts.

Next row (WS): P18 [19: 20: 21: 22], M1P, (P10, M1P) twice, P to end. 59 [61: 63: 65: 67] sts.
Now work in patt as folls:
Row 1 (RS): K9 [10: 11: 12: 13], work next 41 sts as row 1 of chart for sleeve, K to end.
Row 2: P9 [10: 11: 12: 13], work next 41 sts as row 2 of chart for sleeve, P to end.
These 2 rows set the sts – central chart with st st at sides.
Keeping sts correct and repeating the 20 row patt rep throughout, cont as set, shaping sides by inc 1 st at each end of next and every foll 4th row to 103 [105: 107: 109: 111] sts, then on every foll 6th row until there are 109 [113: 117: 121: 125] sts, taking inc sts into st st.
Cont straight until sleeve meas 53 [55: 57: 59: 61] cm, ending with RS facing for next row.

Shape top

Keeping patt correct, cast off 2 [2: 3: 3: 3] sts at beg of next 6 [2: 26: 22: 18] rows, then 3 [3: 4: 4: 4] sts at beg of foll 22 [26: 2: 6: 10] rows. 31 sts.

Shape saddle strap

Left sleeve only

Cast off 10 sts at beg of next row, then 5 sts at beg of foll row. 16 sts.

Right sleeve only

Cast off 5 sts at beg of next row, then 10 sts at beg of foll row. 16 sts.

Both sleeves

Next row (RS): K3, (P2, K2) 3 times, K1.
Next row: K1, (P2, K2) 3 times, P2, K1.

Rep last 2 rows until saddle strap meas 16 [18: 20: 22: 23] cm from last set of cast-off sts, ending at front neck edge. (This is after a RS row for left sleeve, or a WS row for right sleeve.)

Shape neck
Cast off 9 sts at beg of next row. 7 sts.
Dec 1 st at neck (cast-off) edge of next 6 rows.
Fasten off rem st.

MAKING UP
Press as described on the information page.
Join all saddle shoulder and armhole seams using back stitch, or mattress stitch if preferred, as folls: Matching fasten-off point of sleeve saddle strap to marker along back neck edge, sew back row-end edge of saddle strap to back shoulder edge, then sew shaped cast-off edge of sleeve to back armhole edge. In similar way, sew front row-end edge of saddle strap to front shoulder edge, then sew shaped cast-off edge of sleeve to front armhole edge.

Neckband
With RS facing and using 3¼mm (US 3) circular needle, beg and ending at left back saddle shoulder seam, pick up and knit 16 sts from end of left saddle strap (this should be 1 st for each st of saddle strap), 7 sts down left side of neck, 26 [26: 28: 28: 30] sts from front, 7 sts up right side of neck, 16 sts from end of right saddle strap (this should be 1 st for each st of saddle strap), then 28 [28: 30: 30: 32] sts from back (between markers). 100 [100: 104: 104: 108] sts.
Round 1 (RS): P1, *K2, P2, rep from * to last 3 sts, K2, P1.
Rep this round 6 times more.
Cast off in rib.
See information page for finishing instructions.

Body & Sleeve Chart

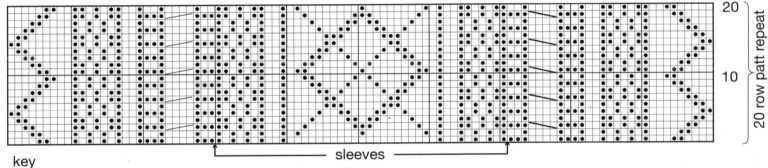

20

10

20 row patt repeat

sleeves

key

□	K on RS, P on WS
▣	P on RS, K on WS
⬚⬚	C4B
⬚⬚	C4F

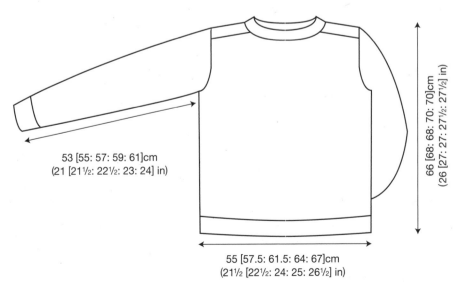

53 [55: 57: 59: 61]cm
(21 [21½: 22½: 23: 24] in)

55 [57.5: 61.5: 64: 67]cm
(21½ [22½: 24: 25: 26½] in)

66 [68: 68: 70: 70]cm
(26 [27: 27: 27½: 27½] in)

oak

main image page 34

SIZE

S	M	L	XL	XXL	
To fit chest					
102	107	112	117	122	cm
40	42	44	46	48	in

YARN

Rowan Purelife Organic Cotton

13	14	15	16	16	x 50gm

(photographed in Quebracho and Cuba 983)

NEEDLES

1 pair 3¼mm (no 10) (US 3) needles
1 pair 3¾mm (no 9) (US 5) needles

FASTENINGS

7 large stud fasteners

TENSION

22 sts and 30 rows to 10 cm measured over st st using 3¾/4mm (US 5) needles.

BACK

Using 3¼mm (US 3) needles cast on 131 [137: 147: 155: 161] sts.
Row 1 (RS): K0 [0: 2: 0: 0], P3 [0: 3: 3: 0], (K3, P3) 4 [5: 5: 6: 7] times, (K2, P1) 25 times, K2, (P3, K3) 4 [5: 5: 6: 7] times, P3 [0: 3: 3: 0], K0 [0: 2: 0: 0].
Row 2: P0 [0: 2: 0: 0], K3 [0: 3: 3: 0], (P3, K3) 4 [5: 5: 6: 7] times, (P2, K1) 25 times, P2, (K3, P3) 4 [5: 5: 6: 7] times, K3 [0: 3: 3: 0], P0 [0: 2: 0: 0].
These 2 rows form rib.
Work in rib for a further 18 rows, ending with RS facing for next row.
Change to 3¾mm (US 5) needles.
Now work in patt as folls:
Row 1 (RS): K0 [0: 2: 0: 0], P3 [0: 3: 3: 0], (K3, P3) 4 [5: 5: 6: 7] times, K77, (P3, K3) 4 [5: 5: 6: 7] times, P3 [0: 3: 3: 0], K0 [0: 2: 0: 0].
Row 2: P0 [0: 2: 0: 0], K3 [0: 3: 3: 0], (P3, K3) 4 [5: 5: 6: 7] times, P77, (K3, P3) 4 [5: 5: 6: 7] times, K3 [0: 3: 3: 0], P0 [0: 2: 0: 0].
These 2 rows form patt.
Cont in patt until back meas 38 [39: 38: 39: 38] cm, ending with **WS** facing for next row.
Next row (WS): P0 [0: 2: 0: 0], (K1, K2tog) 1 [0: 1: 1: 0] times, (P3, K1, K2tog) 4 [5: 5: 6: 7] times, P77, (K1, K2tog, P3) 4 [5: 5: 6: 7] times, (K1, K2tog) 1 [0: 1: 1: 0] times, P0 [0: 2: 0: 0].
121 [127: 135: 141: 147] sts.
Next row: Knit.
Next row: Purl.
Beg with a P row, now work in rev st st as folls:
Work 4 rows, ending with RS facing for next row.
Shape raglan armholes
Cast off 3 sts at beg of next 2 rows.
115 [121: 129: 135: 141] sts.
Dec 1 st at each end of next 1 [1: 5: 7: 9] rows, then on 1 [0: 0: 0: 0] foll 4th row, then on foll 8 [10: 8: 7: 6] alt rows. 95 [99: 103: 107: 111] sts.

Work 1 row, ending with RS facing for next row.
Next row (RS): K2, K2tog, K to last 4 sts, K2tog tbl, K2.
Next row: Purl.
Rep last 2 rows 26 [28: 29: 31: 32] times, ending with RS facing for next row.
Cast off rem 41 [41: 43: 43: 45] sts.

LEFT FRONT

Using 3¼mm (US 3) needles cast on 70 [73: 78: 82: 85] sts.
Row 1 (RS): K0 [0: 2: 0: 0], P3 [0: 3: 3: 0], (K3, P3) 4 [5: 5: 6: 7] times, (K2, P1) 12 times, K7.
Row 2: K1, P6, (K1, P2) 12 times, (K3, P3) 4 [5: 5: 6: 7] times, K3 [0: 3: 3: 0], P0 [0: 2: 0: 0].
These 2 rows form rib.
Work in rib for a further 18 rows, ending with RS facing for next row.
Change to 3¾mm (US 5) needles.
Now work in patt as folls:
Row 1 (RS): K0 [0: 2: 0: 0], P3 [0: 3: 3: 0], (K3, P3) 4 [5: 5: 6: 7] times, K43.
Row 2: K1, P42, (K3, P3) 4 [5: 5: 6: 7] times, K3 [0: 3: 3: 0], P0 [0: 2: 0: 0].
These 2 rows form patt.
Cont in patt until left front meas 38 [39: 38: 39: 38] cm, ending with **WS** facing for next row.
Next row (WS): K1, P42, (K1, K2tog, P3) 4 [5: 5: 6: 7] times, (K1, K2tog) 1 [0: 1: 1: 0] times, P0 [0: 2: 0: 0]. 65 [68: 72: 75: 78] sts.
Next row: Knit.
Next row: K1, P to end.
Next row (RS): P to last 7 sts, K7.
Next row: K1, P6, K to end.
These 2 rows set the sts.
Cont as set for a further 2 rows, ending with RS facing for next row.

Shape raglan armhole
Keeping sts correct as set, cast off 3 sts at beg of next row. 62 [65: 69: 72: 75] sts.
Work 1 row.
Dec 1 st at raglan armhole edge of next 1 [1: 5: 7: 9] rows, then on 1 [0: 0: 0: 0] foll 4th row, then on foll 8 [10: 8: 7: 6] alt rows. 52 [54: 56: 58: 60] sts.
Work 1 row, ending with RS facing for next row.
Next row (RS): K2, K2tog, K to end.
Next row: K1, P to end.
Rep last 2 rows 15 [17: 17: 19: 19] times more, ending with RS facing for next row. 36 [36: 38: 38: 40] sts.
Shape neck
Next row (RS): K2, K2tog, K to last 15 sts and turn, leaving rem 14 sts on a holder. 20 [20: 22: 22: 24] sts.
Dec 1 st at neck edge of next 8 rows, then on foll 2 [2: 3: 3: 4] alt rows **and at same time** dec 1 st at raglan armhole edge as set on 2nd and every foll alt row. 4 sts.
Next row (WS): P4.
Next row: K1, sl 1, K2tog, psso.
Next row: P2.
Next row: K2tog and fasten off.

RIGHT FRONT

Using 3¼mm (US 3) needles cast on 70 [73: 78: 82: 85] sts.
Row 1 (RS): K7, (P1, K2) 12 times, (P3, K3) 4 [5: 5: 6: 7] times, P3 [0: 3: 3: 0], K0 [0: 2: 0: 0].
Row 2: P0 [0: 2: 0: 0], K3 [0: 3: 3: 0], (P3, K3) 4 [5: 5: 6: 7] times, (P2, K1) 12 times, P6, K1.
These 2 rows form rib.
Work in rib for a further 18 rows, ending with RS facing for next row.
Change to 3¾mm (US 5) needles.
Now work in patt as folls:
Row 1 (RS): K43, (P3, K3) 4 [5: 5: 6: 7] times, P3 [0: 3: 3: 0], K0 [0: 2: 0: 0].

Row 2: P0 [0: 2: 0: 0], K3 [0: 3: 3: 0], (P3, K3) 4 [5: 5: 6: 7] times, P42, K1.
These 2 rows form patt.
Cont in patt until right front meas 38 [39: 38: 39: 38] cm, ending with WS facing for next row.
Next row (WS): P0 [0: 2: 0: 0], (K1, K2tog) 1 [0: 1: 1: 0] times, (P3, K1, K2tog) 4 [5: 5: 6: 7] times, P42, K1. 65 [68: 72: 75: 78] sts.
Next row: Knit.
Next row: P to last st, K1.
Next row (RS): K7, P to end.
Next row: K to last 7 sts, P6, K1.
These 2 rows set the sts.
Cont as set for a further 3 rows, ending with WS facing for next row.

Shape raglan armhole
Keeping sts correct as set, cast off 3 sts at beg of next row. 62 [65: 69: 72: 75] sts.
Dec 1 st at raglan armhole edge of next 1 [1: 5: 7: 9] rows, then on 1 [0: 0: 0: 0] foll 4th row, then on foll 8 [10: 8: 7: 6] alt rows. 52 [54: 56: 58: 60] sts.
Work 1 row, ending with RS facing for next row.
Next row (RS): K to last 4 sts, K2tog tbl, K2.
Next row: P to last st, K1.
Rep last 2 rows 15 [17: 17: 19: 19] times more, ending with RS facing for next row. 36 [36: 38: 38: 40] sts.

Shape neck
Next row (RS): K15 and slip these sts onto a holder, K to last 4 sts, K2tog tbl, K2. 20 [20: 22: 22: 24] sts.
Dec 1 st at neck edge of next 8 rows, then on foll 2 [2: 3: 3: 4] alt rows and at same time dec 1 st at raglan armhole edge as set on 2nd and every foll alt row. 4 sts.
Next row (WS): P4.
Next row: K3tog, K1.
Next row: P2.
Next row: K2tog and fasten off.

SLEEVES
Using 3¼mm (US 3) needles cast on 51 [53: 55: 57: 59] sts.
Row 1 (RS): K0 [1: 2: 0: 1], (P1, K2) 5 [5: 5: 6: 6] times, (P3, K3) 3 times, P3, (K2, P1) 5 [5: 5: 6: 6] times, K0 [1: 2: 0: 1].
Row 2: P0 [1: 2: 0: 1], (K1, P2) 5 [5: 5: 6: 6] times, (K3, P3) 3 times, K3, (P2, K1) 5 [5: 5: 6: 6] times, P0 [1: 2: 0: 1].
These 2 rows form rib.
Work in rib for a further 18 rows, ending with RS facing for next row.
Change to 3¾mm (US 5) needles.
Row 1 (RS): K15 [16: 17: 18: 19], (P3, K3) 3 times, P3, K to end.
Row 2: P15 [16: 17: 18: 19], (K3, P3) 3 times, K3, P to end.
These 2 rows form patt.
Cont in patt, shaping sides by inc 1 st at each end of next and every foll 4th row to 105 [107: 103: 105: 101] sts, then on every foll 6th row until there are 111 [115: 117: 121: 123] sts, taking inc sts into st st.
Cont straight until sleeve meas 53 [55: 57: 59: 61] cm, ending with RS facing for next row.

Shape raglan
Keeping patt correct, cast off 3 sts at beg of next 2 rows. 105 [109: 111: 115: 117] sts.
Next row (RS): K2, K2tog, patt to last 4 sts, K2tog tbl, K2.
Next row: P2, P2tog tbl, patt to last 4 sts, P2tog, P2.
Next row: K2, K2tog, patt to last 4 sts, K2tog tbl, K2. 99 [103: 105: 109: 111] sts.
Next row: Patt.
Rep last 2 rows until 33 sts rem, ending with RS facing for next row.

Left sleeve only
Dec 1 st at each end of next row, then cast off 7 sts at beg of foll row. 24 sts.
Dec 1 st at beg of next row, then cast off 8 sts at beg of foll row. 15 sts.
Rep last 2 rows once more.

Right sleeve only
Cast off 8 sts at beg and dec 1 st at end of next row. 24 sts.
Work 1 row.
Rep last 2 rows twice more.

Both sleeves
Cast off rem 6 sts.

MAKING UP
Press as described on the information page.
Join all raglan seams using back stitch, or mattress stitch if preferred.

Collar
With RS facing and using 3¼mm (US 3) needles, slip 15 sts from right front holder onto right needle, rejoin yarn and pick up and knit 13 [13: 16: 16: 19] sts up right side of neck, 27 sts from top of right sleeve (this should be 1 st for each of the 21 centre rib sts and 3 sts at each side), 41 [41: 44: 44: 44] sts from back, 27 sts from top of left sleeve (this should be 1 st for each of the 21 centre rib sts and 3 sts at each side), and 13 [13: 16: 16: 19] sts down left side of neck, then patt 15 sts from left front holder. 151 [151: 160: 160: 166] sts.
Row 1 (WS): K1, P6, (K1, P2) 8 [8: 9: 9: 10] times, K3, (P3, K3) 3 times, (P2, K1) 15 [15: 16: 16: 16] times, P2, (K3, P3) 3 times, K3, (P2, K1) 8 [8: 9: 9: 10] times, P6, K1.
Row 2: K7, (P1, K2) 8 [8: 9: 9: 10] times, P3, (K3, P3) 3 times, (K2, P1) 15 [15: 16: 16: 16] times, K2, (P3, K3) 3 times, P3, (K2, P1) 8 [8: 9: 9: 10] times, K7.
These 2 rows form rib.
Rep last 3 rows until collar meas 8 cm from pick-up row, ending with RS facing for next row.
Cast off in rib.

Front facings (both alike)
With RS facing and using 3¼mm (US 3) needles, pick up and knit 116 [120: 118: 122: 120] sts evenly along entire front opening edge, between cast-on edge and top of collar.
Beg with a P row, work in st st for 8 rows, ending with **WS** facing for next row.
Cast off purlwise (on **WS**).
Fold front facings to inside along pick-up row and slip stitch in place.
See information page for finishing instructions. Attach press fasteners to fasten front so that opening edges over lap by 7 sts.

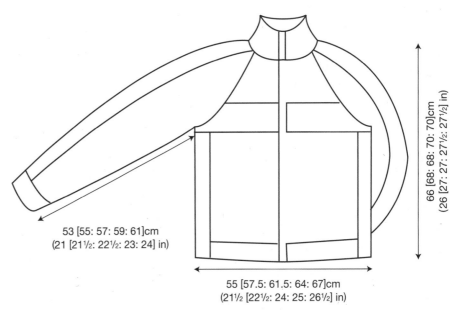

53 [55: 57: 59: 61]cm
(21 [21½: 22½: 23: 24] in)

55 [57.5: 61.5: 64: 67]cm
(21½ [22½: 24: 25: 26½] in)

66 [68: 68: 70: 70]cm
(26 [27: 27: 27½: 27½] in)

ash

main image page 29

SIZE

S	M	L	XL	XXL	
To fit chest					
102	107	112	117	122	cm
40	42	44	46	48	in

YARN

Rowan Purelife Organic Cotton

9	10	11	12	12	x 50gm

(photographed in Natural 986)

NEEDLES

1 pair 3¹/4mm (no 10) (US 3) needles
1 pair 4mm (no 8) (US 6) needles
Cable needle

TENSION

20 sts and 29 rows to 10 cm measured over patt using 4mm (US 6) needles.

BACK

Using 3¹/4mm (US 3) needles cast on 121 [127: 136: 142: 148] sts.
Row 1 (RS): P1, *K2, P1, rep from * to end.
Row 2: K1, *P2, K1, rep from * to end.
These 2 rows form rib.
Work in rib for a further 18 rows, dec 0 [0: 1: 1: 1] st at end of last row and ending with RS facing for next row. 121 [127: 135: 141: 147] sts.
Change to 4mm (US 6) needles.
Now work in patt as folls:
Row 1 (RS): Knit.
Row 2: Purl.
Row 3: Knit.
Rows 4 and 5: Purl.
Row 6: Knit.
These 6 rows form patt.
Cont in patt until back meas 41 [42: 41: 42: 41] cm, ending with RS facing for next row.
Shape armholes
Place markers at both ends of last row to denote base of armholes.
Keeping patt correct, dec 1 st at each end of next 5 [3: 3: 3: 1] rows, then on foll 3 [3: 3: 1: 2] alt rows. 105 [115: 123: 133: 141] sts.
Cont straight until armhole meas 23 [24: 25: 26: 27] cm, ending with RS facing for next row.
Shape back neck
Next row (RS): Patt 37 [42: 45: 50: 53] sts and turn, leaving rem sts on a holder.
Work each side of neck separately.
Keeping patt correct, dec 1 st at neck edge of next row,

ending with RS facing for next row.
36 [41: 44: 49: 52] sts.
Shape shoulder
Cast off 11 [13: 14: 15: 16] sts at beg of next and foll alt row **and at same time** dec 1 st at neck edge of next 3 rows.
Work 1 row.
Cast off rem 11 [12: 13: 16: 17] sts.
With RS facing, rejoin yarn to rem sts, cast off centre 31 [31: 33: 33: 35] sts, patt to end.
Complete to match first side, reversing shapings.

FRONT

Work as given for back until 42 [42: 44: 44: 46] rows less have been worked than on back to beg of shoulder shaping, ending with RS facing for next row.
Divide for front opening
Next row (RS): Patt 50 [55: 59: 64: 68] sts and turn, leaving rem sts on a holder.
Work each side of neck separately.
Work 22 rows, ending with **WS** facing for next row.
Shape neck
Keeping patt correct, cast off 7 sts at beg of next row. 43 [48: 52: 57: 61] sts.
Dec 1 st at neck edge of next 7 rows, then on foll 2 [2: 3: 3: 4] alt rows, then on foll 4th row.
33 [38: 41: 46: 49] sts.
Work 3 rows, ending with RS facing for next row.
Shape shoulder
Cast off 11 [13: 14: 15: 16] sts at beg of next and foll alt row.
Work 1 row.
Cast off rem 11 [12: 13: 16: 17] sts.

With RS facing, rejoin yarn to rem sts, cast off centre 5 sts, patt to end.
Complete to match first side, reversing shapings.

MAKING UP

Press as described on the information page.
Join both shoulder seams using back stitch, or mattress stitch if preferred.
Front bands (both alike)
With RS facing and using 3¹/4mm (US 3) needles, pick up and knit 19 sts along row-end edge of front opening, between cast-off sts at base of opening and beg of neck shaping.
Row 1 (WS): K1, *P2, K1, rep from * to end.
Row 2: K3, *P1, K2, rep from * to last st, K1.
These 2 rows form rib.
Work in rib for a further 5 rows, ending with RS facing for next row.
Cast off in rib.
Lay left front band over right front band and sew row-end edges to cast-off sts at base of opening.
Collar
Using 3¹/4mm (US 3) needles cast on 121 [121: 127: 127: 136] sts.
Beg with row 2, work in rib as given for front bands for 7 cm, ending with RS facing for next row.
Cast off 4 [4: 4: 4: 5] sts at beg of next 6 [6: 4: 4: 12] rows, then 5 [5: 5: 5: 6] sts at beg of foll 10 [10: 12: 12: 4] rows.
Cast off rem 47 [47: 51: 51: 52] sts.
Slip stitch shaped cast-off edge of collar to neck edge, matching row-end edges of collar to cast-off edge of front bands.

Armhole borders (both alike)
With RS facing and using 3¼mm (US 3) needles, pick up and knit 112 [116: 120: 124: 130] sts evenly all round armhole edge.
Work in g st for 4 rows, ending with WS facing for next row.
Cast off knitwise (on **WS**).
See information page for finishing instructions.

67 [69: 69: 71: 71]cm
(26½ [27: 27: 28: 28] in)

60.5 [63.5: 67.5: 70.5: 73.5]cm
(24 [25: 26½: 28: 29] in)

cornflower
main image page 27

SIZE

	S	M	L	XL	
To fit bust					
	81-86	91-97	102-107	112-117	cm
	32-34	36-38	40-42	44-46	in

YARN
Rowan Purelife Organic Cotton

14	15	18	20	x 50gm

(photographed in Logwood 981)

NEEDLES
1 pair 3¾mm (no 9) (US 5) needles

TENSION
23 sts and 38 rows to 10 cm measured over moss st using 3¾mm (US 5) needles.

BACK
Using 3¾mm (US 5) needles cast on 109 [121: 135: 149] sts.
Row 1 (RS): K1, *P1, K1, rep from * to end.
Row 2: As row 1.
These 2 rows form moss st.
Cont in patt until back meas 12 cm, ending with RS facing for next row.
Dec 1 st at each end of next and every foll 20th row until 99 [111: 125: 139] sts rem.
Cont straight until back meas 48 [49: 50: 51] cm,
ending with RS facing for next row.
Shape armholes
Keeping moss st correct, cast off 3 [4: 5: 6] sts at beg of next 2 rows. 93 [103: 115: 127] sts.**
Dec 1 st at each end of next 3 [5: 7: 9] rows, then on foll 3 [4: 4: 5] alt rows. 81 [85: 93: 99] sts.
Cont straight until armhole meas 18 [19: 20: 21] cm, ending with RS facing for next row.
Shape back neck
Next row (RS): Moss st 24 [26: 29: 32] sts and turn, leaving rem sts on a holder.
Work each side of neck separately.
Keeping moss st correct, dec 1 st at neck edge of next 3 rows. 21 [23: 26: 29] sts.
Shape shoulder
Cast off 6 [7: 8: 9] sts at beg and dec 1 st at end of next row.
Work 1 row.
Rep last 2 rows once more.
Cast off rem 7 [7: 8: 9] sts.
With RS facing, rejoin yarn to rem sts, cast off centre 33 [33: 35: 35] sts, moss st to end.

Complete to match first side, reversing shapings.

FRONT

Work as given for back to **.

Dec 1 st at each end of next 0 [4: 6: 9] rows.
93 [95: 103: 109] sts.

Work 0 [0: 0: 1] row, ending with RS facing for next row.

Divide for front opening

Next row (RS): Work 2 tog, moss st 44 [45: 49: 52] sts and turn, leaving rem sts on a holder.

Work each side of neck separately.

Keeping moss st correct, dec 1 st at armhole edge of next [2nd: 2nd: 2nd] and foll 1 [0: 0: 0] rows, then on foll 3 alt rows. 40 [42: 46: 49] sts.

Cont straight until 31 [31: 33: 33] rows less have been worked than on back to beg of shoulder shaping, ending with WS facing for next row.

Shape neck

Keeping moss st correct, cast off 8 sts at beg of next row. 32 [34: 38: 41] sts.

Dec 1 st at neck edge of next 7 rows, then on foll 3 [3: 4: 4] alt rows, then on 3 foll 4th rows.
19 [21: 24: 27] sts.

Work 5 rows, ending with RS facing for next row.

Shape shoulder

Cast off 6 [7: 8: 9] sts at beg of next and foll alt row.

Work 1 row.

Cast off rem 7 [7: 8: 9] sts.

With RS facing, rejoin yarn to rem sts, work 2 tog, moss st to last 2 sts, work 2 tog.

Complete to match first side, reversing shapings.

SLEEVES

Using 3¾mm (US 5) needles cast on 61 [63: 65: 65] sts.

Work in moss st as given for back, shaping sides by inc 1 st at each end of 9th [9th: 7th: 7th] and every foll 10th [10th: 8th: 8th] row to 81 [91: 69: 89] sts, then on every foll 12th [12th: 10th: 10th] row until there are 89 [93: 97: 101] sts.

Cont straight until sleeve meas 44 [45: 46: 46] cm, ending with RS facing for next row.

Shape top

Keeping moss st correct, cast off 3 [4: 5: 6] sts at beg of next 2 rows. 83 [85: 87: 89] sts.

Dec 1 st at each end of next 5 rows, then on every foll alt row to 55 sts, then on foll 11 rows, ending with RS facing for next row. 33 sts.

Cast off 6 sts at beg of next 2 rows.

Cast off rem 21 sts.

MAKING UP

Press as described on the information page.

Join both shoulder seams using back stitch, or mattress stitch if preferred.

See information page for finishing instructions, setting in sleeves using the set-in method and leaving side seams open for first 10 cm.

Belt

Using 3¾mm (US 5) needles cast on 13 sts.

Work in moss st as given for back until belt meas 100 [110: 120: 130] cm, ending with RS facing for next row.

Cast off.

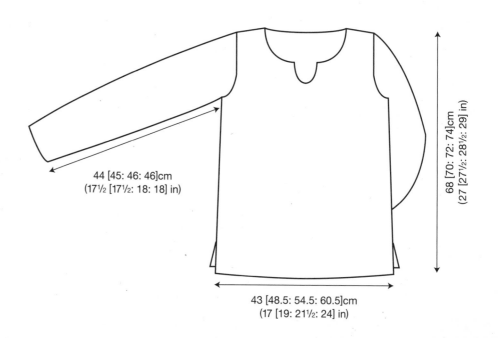

44 [45: 46: 46]cm
(17½ [17½: 18: 18] in)

68 [70: 72: 74]cm
(27 [27½: 28½: 29] in)

43 [48.5: 54.5: 60.5]cm
(17 [19: 21½: 24] in)

Information

Tension

Obtaining the correct tension is perhaps the single factor which can make the difference between a successful garment and a disastrous one. It controls both the shape and size of an article, so any variation, however slight, can distort the finished garment. Different designers feature in our books and it is their tension, given at the start of each pattern, which you must match. We recommend that you knit a square in pattern and/or stocking stitch (depending on the pattern instructions) of perhaps 5 – 10 more stitches and 5 – 10 more rows than those given in the tension note. Mark out the central 10cm square with pins. If you have too many stitches to 10cm try again using thicker needles, if you have too few stitches to 10cm try again using finer needles. Once you have achieved the correct tension your garment will be knitted to the measurements indicated in the size diagram shown at the end of the pattern.

Sizing and Size Diagram Note

The instructions are given for the smallest size. Where they vary, work the figures in brackets for the larger sizes. **One set of figures refers to all sizes**. Included with most patterns in this brochure is a **'size diagram'**, or sketch of the finished garment and its dimensions. To help you choose the size of garment to knit please refer to the **new** sizing guide on page 40.

Chart Note

Many of the patterns in the book are worked from charts. Each square on a chart represents a stitch and each line of squares a row of knitting. Each colour used is given a different letter and these are shown in the materials section, or in the **key** alongside the chart of each pattern.

When working from the charts, read odd rows (K) from right to left and even rows (P) from left to right, unless otherwise stated.

Finishing Instructions

After working for hours knitting a garment, it seems a great pity that many garments are spoiled because such little care is taken in the pressing and finishing process. Follow the following tips for a truly professional looking garment.

Pressing

Block out each piece of knitting and following the instructions on the ball band press the garment pieces, omitting the ribs.

Tip

Take special care to press the edges, as this will make sewing up both easier and neater. If the ball band indicates that the fabric is not to be pressed, then covering the blocked out fabric with a damp white cotton cloth and leaving it to stand will have the desired effect. Darn in all ends neatly along the selvage edge or a colour join, as appropriate.

Stitching

When stitching the pieces together, remember to match areas of colour and texture very carefully where they meet. Use a seam stitch such as back stitch or mattress stitch for all main knitting seams and join all ribs and neckband with mattress stitch, unless otherwise stated.

Construction

Having completed the pattern instructions, join left shoulder and neckband seams as detailed above. Sew the top of the sleeve to the body of the garment using the method detailed in the pattern, referring to the appropriate guide:

Straight cast-off sleeves

Place centre of cast-off edge of sleeve to shoulder seam. Sew top of sleeve to body, using markers as guidelines where applicable.

Square set-in sleeves

Place centre of cast-off edge of sleeve to shoulder seam. Set sleeve head into armhole, the straight sides at top of sleeve to form a neat rightangle to cast-off sts at armhole on back and front.

Shallow set-in sleeves

Place centre of cast off edge of sleeve to shoulder seam. Match decreases at beg of armhole shaping to decreases at top of sleeve. Sew sleeve head into armhole, easing in shapings.

Set-in sleeves

Place centre of cast-off edge of sleeve to shoulder seam. Set in sleeve, easing sleeve head into armhole.

Join side and sleeve seams.

Slip stitch pocket edgings and linings into place.

Sew on buttons to correspond with buttonholes.

Ribbed welts and neckbands and any areas of garter stitch should not be pressed.

Working a Lace Pattern

When working a lace pattern it is important to remember that if you are unable to work both the increase and corresponding decrease and vica versa, the stitches should be worked in stocking stitch.

Abbreviations

K	knit	**RS**	right side	
P	purl	**WS**	wrong side	
st(s)	stitch(es)	**sl 1**	slip one stitch	
inc	increas(e)(ing)	**psso**	pass slipped stitch over	
dec	decreas(e)(ing)	**p2sso**	pass 2 slipped stitches over	
st st	stocking stitch (1 row K, 1 row P)	**tbl**	through back of loop	
g st	garter stitch (K every row)	**M1**	make one stitch by picking up horizontal loop before next stitch and knitting into back of it	
beg	begin(ning)			
foll	following	**M1P**	make one stitch by picking up horizontal loop before next stitch and purling into back of it	
rem	remain(ing)			
rev st st	reverse stocking stitch (1 row K, 1 row P)			
rep	repeat	**yfwd**	yarn forward	
alt	alternate	**yrn**	yarn round needle	
cont	continue	**meas**	measures	
patt	pattern	**0**	no stitches, times or rows	
tog	together	**-**	no stitches, times or rows for that size	
mm	millimetres	**yon**	yarn over needle	
cm	centimetres	**yfrn**	yarn forward round needle	
in(s)	inch(es)	**wyib**	with yarn at back	

Crochet Terms

UK crochet terms and abbreviations have been used throughout. The list below gives the US equivalent where they vary.

ABBREV.	UK	US
dc	double crochet	single crochet
htr	half treble	half double crochet
tr	treble	double crochet
dtr	double treble	treble
ttr	triple treble	double treble
qtr	quadruple treble	triple treble

Experience Ratings

Easy, straight forward knitting

Suitable for the average knitter

For the more experienced knitter

Stockists

Australia
Australian Country Spinners,
314 Albert Street, Brunswick, Victoria 3056
Tel: (61) 3 9380 3888
Fax: (61) 3 9387 2674
Email: sales@auspinners.com.au

Austria
Coats Harlander GmbH,
Autokaderstrasse 31, A -1210 Wien
Tel: (01) 27716 – 0
Fax: (01) 27716 - 228

Canada
Westminster Fibres Inc, 165 Ledge Street,
Nashua, New Hampshire 03060
Tel: (1 603) 886 5041/5043
Fax: (1 603) 886 1056
Email: rowan@westminsterfibres.com

China
Coats Shanghai Ltd,
No 9 Building, Baosheng Road,
Songjiang Industrial Zone, Shanghai.
Tel: (86- 21) 5774 3733
Fax: (86-21) 5774 3768

Denmark
Coats Danmark A/S,
Nannasgade 28, 2200 Kobenhavn N.
Tel: (45) 35 86 90 50
Fax: (45) 35 82 15 10
Email: info@hpgruppen.dk
Internet: www.hpgruppen.dk

Finland
Coats Opti Oy, Ketjutie 3, 04220 Kerava
Tel: (358) 9 274 871
Fax: (358) 9 2748 7330
Email: coatsopti.sales@coats.com

France
Coats France / Steiner Frères, 100,
avenue du Général de Gaulle, 18 500
Mehun-Sur-Yèvre
Tel: (33) 02 48 23 12 30
Fax: (33) 02 48 23 12 40

Germany
Coats GMbH, Kaiserstrasse 1
D-79341 Kenzingen
Tel: (49) 7644 8020
Fax: (49) 7644 802399
Internet: www.coatsgmbh.de

Holland, Belgium and Luxembourg
Coats Benelux, Ring Oost 14A,
Ninove, 9400, Belgium
Tel: 0346 35 37 00
Email: sales.coatsninove@coats.com

Hong Kong
Coats China Holdings Ltd, 19/F
Millennium City 2, 378 Kwun Tong Road, Kwun
Tong, Kowloon
Tel: (852) 2798 6886
Fax: (852) 2305 0311

Iceland
Storkurinn, Laugavegi 59, 101 Reykjavik
Tel: (354) 551 8258
Email: malin@mmedia.is

Italy
D.L. srl,Via Piave, 24 – 26, 20016 Pero, Milan
Tel: (39) 02 339 10 180
Fax: (39) 02 339 14 661

Japan
Puppy-Jardin Co Ltd, 3-8-11 Kudanminami
Chiyodaku, Hiei Kudan Bldg. 5F, Tokyo
Tel: (81) 3 3222-7076
Fax: (81) 3 3222-7066
Email: info@rowan-jaeger.com

Korea
Coats Korea Co Ltd, 5F Kuckdong B/D,
935-40 Bangbae- Dong,
Seocho-Gu, Seoul
Tel: (82) 2 521 6262
Fax: (82) 2 521 5181

Lebanon
y.knot, Saifi Village, Mkhalissiya Street 162, Beirut
Tel: (961) 1 992211.
Fax: (961) 1 315553
Email: y.knot@cyberia.net.lb

New Zealand
ACS New Zealand
1 March Place, Belfast, Christchurch
Tel: 64-3-323-6665
Fax: 64-3-323-6660

Norway
Coats Knappehuset AS, Pb 100 Ulset,
5873 Bergen
Tel: (47) 55 53 93 00
Fax: (47) 55 53 93 93

Singapore
Golden Dragon Store, 101 Upper
Cross Street #02-51, People's Park Centre,
Singapore 058357
Tel: (65) 6 5358454
Fax: (65) 6 2216278
Email: gdscraft@hotmail.com

South Africa
Arthur Bales PTY, PO Box 44644, Linden 2104
Tel: (27) 11 888 2401
Fax: (27) 11 782 6137

Spain
Oyambre, Pau Claris 145, 80009 Barcelona
Tel: (34) 670 011957
Fax: (34) 93 4872672
Email: oyambre@oyambreonline.com

Sweden
Coats Expotex AB, Division Craft, Box 297,
401 24 Goteborg
Tel: (46) 33 720 79 00
Fax: 46 31 47 16 50

Switzerland
Coats Stroppel AG, CH -5300 Turgi (AG)
Tel: (41) 562981220
Fax: (41) 56 298 12 50

Taiwan
Cactus Quality Co Ltd, PO Box 30 485, Taipei,
Taiwan, ROC
Office: 7FL-2, No 140, Roosevelt Road, Sec2,
Taipei, ROC
Tel: 886-2-23656527
Fax: 886-2-23656503
Email: cqcl@m17.hinet.net

USA
Westminster Fibers Inc, 165 Ledge Street,
Nashua, New Hampshire 03060
Tel: (1 603) 886 5041/5043
Fax: (1 603) 886 1056
Email: rowan@westminsterfibers.com

UK
Rowan, Green Lane Mill, Holmfirth,
West Yorkshire, England, HD9 2DX
Tel: +44 (0) 1484 681881
Fax: +44 (0) 1484 687920
Email: mail@knitrowan.com
Internet: www.knitrowan.com

**For stockists in all other countries please
contact Rowan for details.**

Photographer: Moy Williams

Styling: Marie Wallin **Assisted by:** Sarah Hatton

Art Direction: Marie Wallin

Hair and Make-up: Frances Prescott

Design Layout: 10 Associates Ltd, 6a Cartwright Court, Bradley Business Park, Dyson Wood Way, Huddersfield, HD2 1GN

Models: Amy Griffiths – Excel Models, Christian Lambelin – Select Model Management, Edie Hughes – Kids London

Location: Many thanks to Patrick and Lucy of Odessa Farm, Wood Dalling, Norfolk – Light Locations

With special thanks to the following handknitters:

Ann Banks, Carole Bayliss, Joan Broadbent, Judith Chamberlain, Joyce Coop, Margaret Goddard, Susan Grimes, Glennis Garnett, Honey Ingram, Elizabeth Jones, Audrey Kidd, Joyce Limon, Andrea McHugh, Yvonne Rawlinson, Arna Ronan, Wendy Shipman, Wendy Stevens

First published in Great Britain in 2008 by Rowan Yarns Ltd, Green Lane Mill, Holmfirth, West Yorkshire, England, HD9 2DX

Internet: www.knitrowan.com

© Copyright Rowan 2008

British Library Cataloguing in Publication Data Rowan Yarns – Rowan Purelife The Organic Cotton Collection

ISBN 978-1-906007-02-7